GRATEFUL DEAD AUTHENTIC GUITAR

Grateful Dead

BERTHA . . . 2
CHINA CAT SUNFLOWER . . . 26
DARK STAR . . . 36
DIRE WOLF . . . 13
GOING DOWN THE ROAD FEELIN' BAD . . . 60
I KNOW YOU RIDER . . . 40
ME AND MY UNCLE . . . 52
ONE MORE SATURDAY NIGHT . . . 71
PLAYING IN THE BAND . . . 84
ST. STEPHEN . . . 91
SUGAREE . . . 106
TENNESSEE JED . . . 112
TOUCH OF GREY . . . 125

Artwork © Grateful Dead Productions, Inc.
Editor: Aaron Stang
Transcribed by: Hemme Luttjeboer

©1996 ICE NINE PUBLISHING CO., INC.
All Rights Reserved

Any duplication, adaptation or arrangement of the compositions
contained in this collection requires the written consent of the Publisher.
No part of this book may be photocopied or reproduced in any way without permission.
Unauthorized uses are an infringement of U.S. Copyright Act and are punishable by Law.

BERTHA

Words by ROBERT HUNTER
Music by JERRY GARCIA

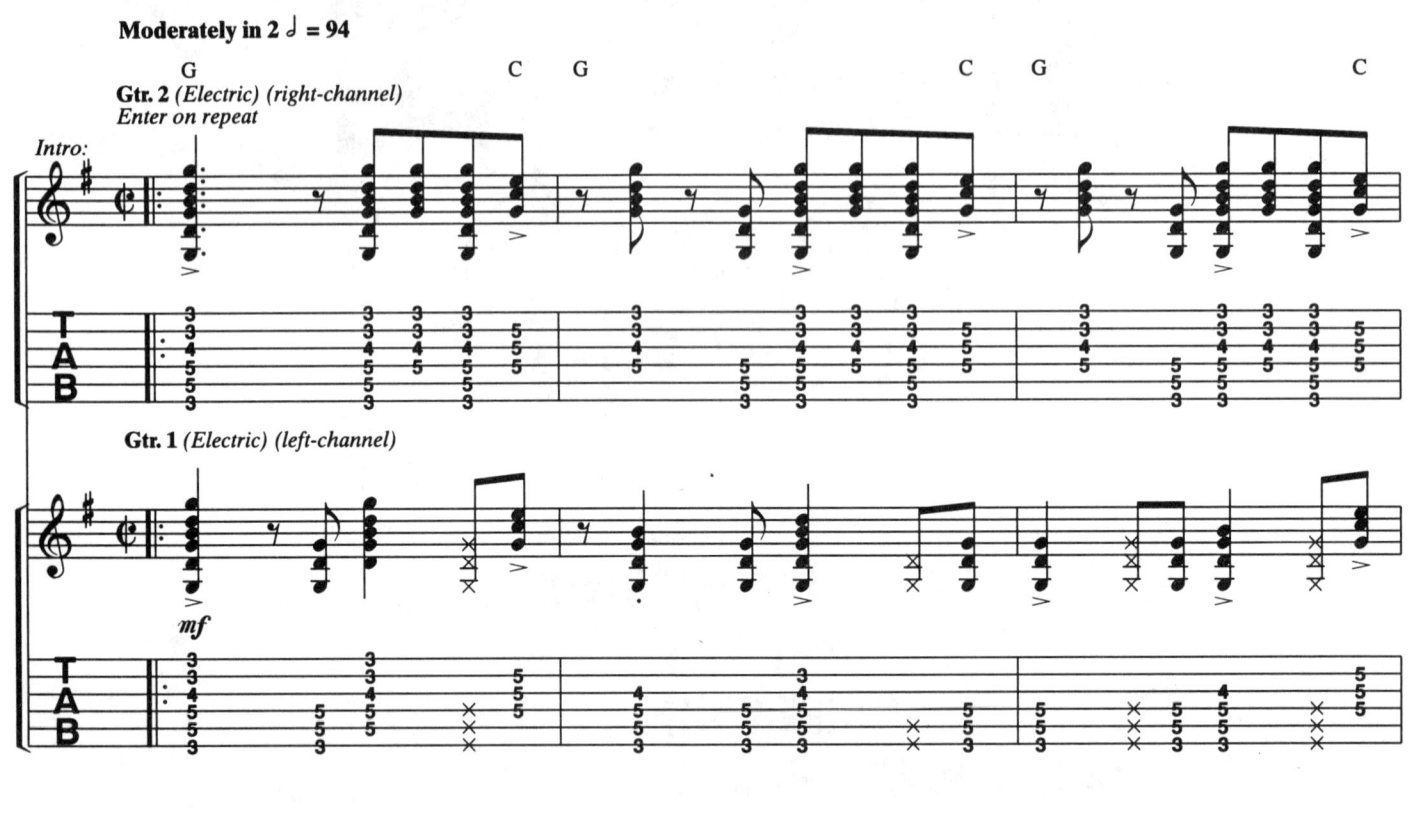

Bertha - 11 - 1
PG9557

© 1971 ICE NINE PUBLISHING CO., INC.
This Arrangement © 1996 ICE NINE PUBLISHING CO., INC.
All Rights Reserved

10

Bertha - 11 - 9
PG9557

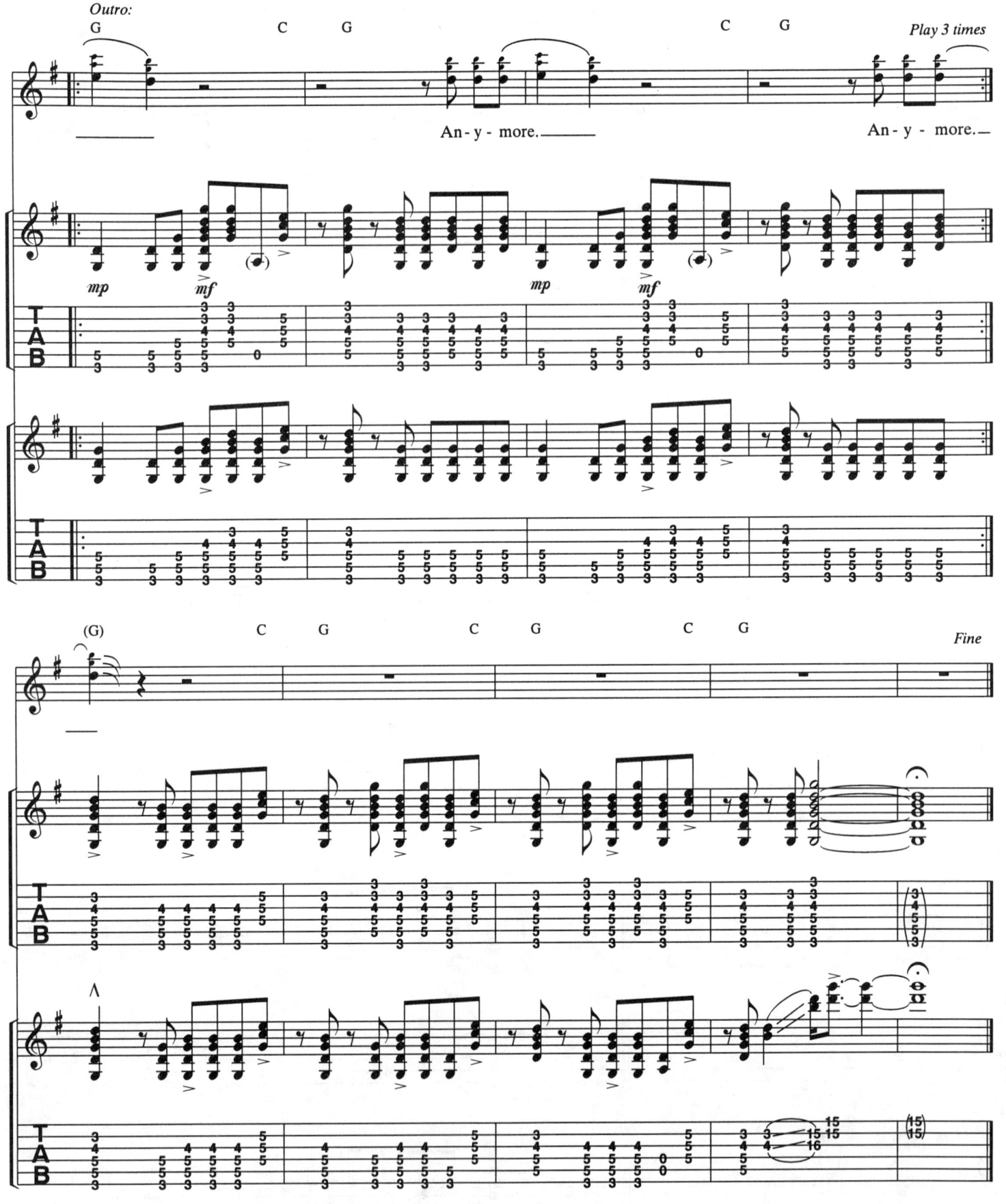

Verse 2:
Dressed myself in green.
Lord, I went down into the sea.
Try to see what's goin' down.
Try to read between the lines.
I had a feelin' I was fallin', fallin', fallin'.
I turned around to see,
Heard a voice callin',
Lord, you was comin' after me.

Verse 3:
Ran into a rainstorm.
Ducked into a bar door.
It's all night pourin', pourin' rain.
Lord, but not a drop on me.
Test me, test me, test me, test me.
Why don't you arrest me?
Throw me in the jail house,
Lord, until the sun go down.

DIRE WOLF

Words by ROBERT HUNTER
Music by JERRY GARCIA

18

Dire Wolf - 13 - 6
PG9557

E
hold
hold
hold
hold
D
E
A
C♯7
F♯m
E
Oo,
oo,
oo.
8va
hold bend
hold
hold

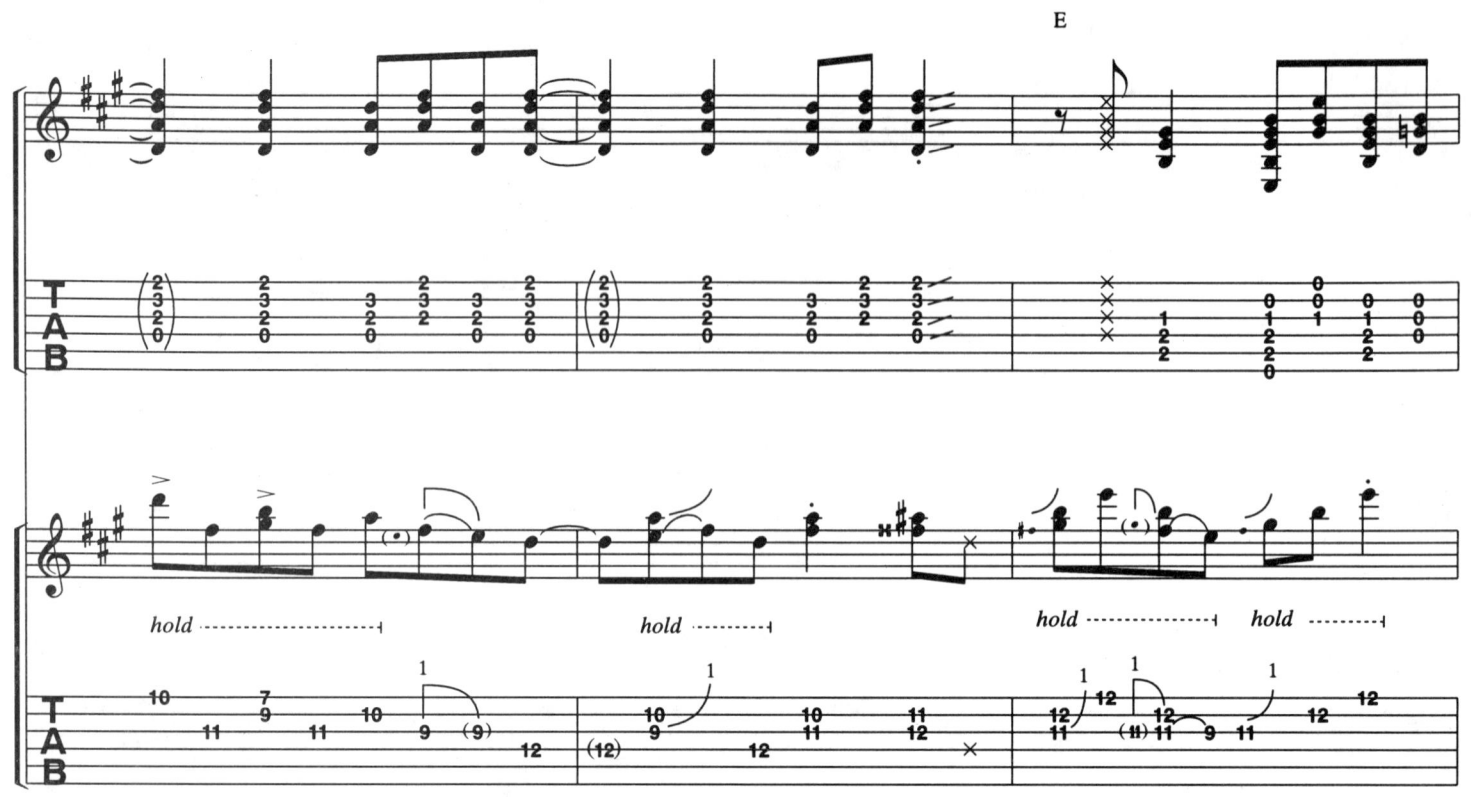

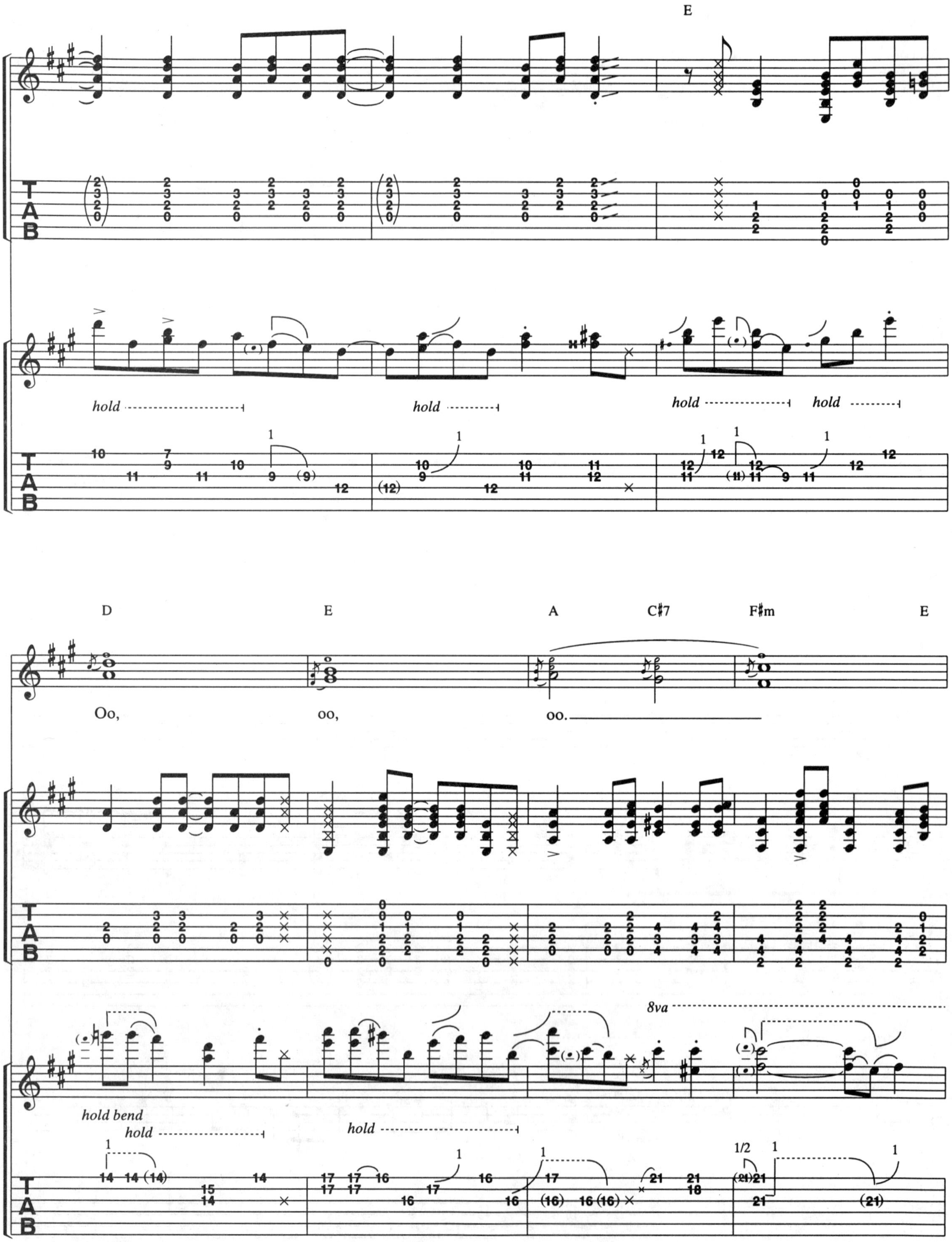

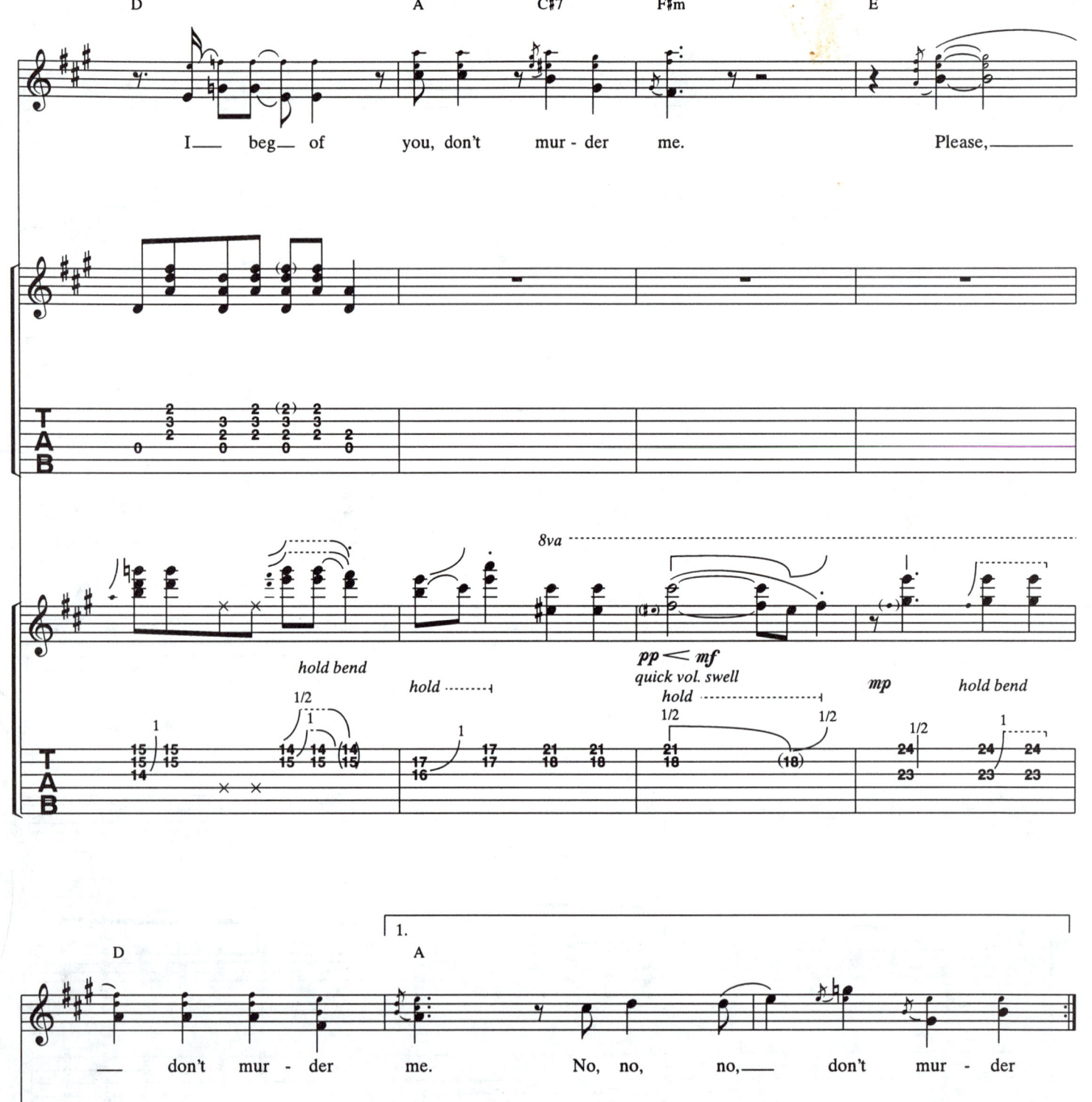

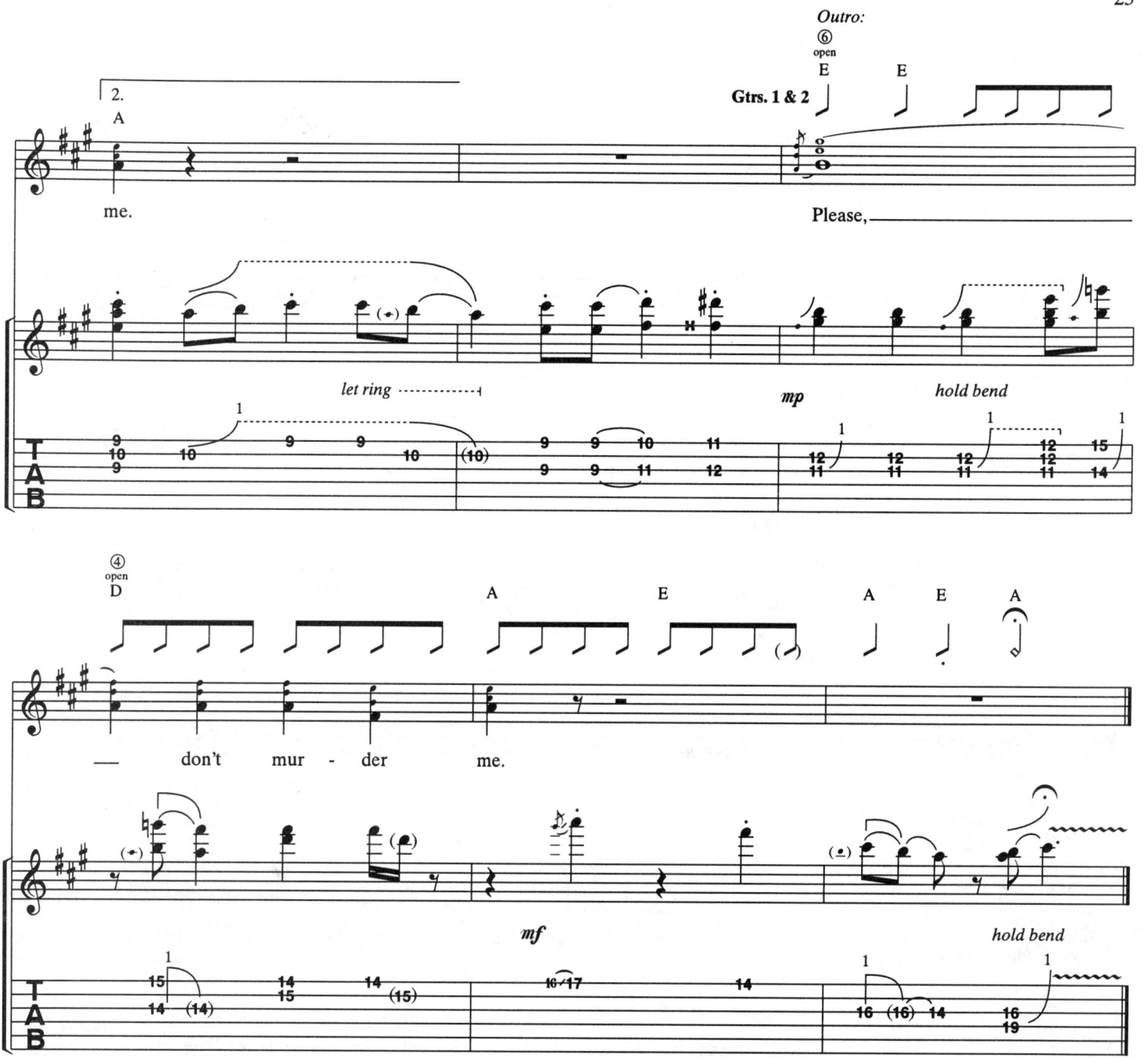

Verse 4:
The wolf came in, I got my cards,
We sat down for a game.
I cut my deck to the queen of hearts
But the cards were all the same;
Don't murder me...
(To Chorus:)

Verse 5:
In the back-wash of Fennario,
The black and bloody mire,
The dire wolf collects his due
While the boys sing around the fire:
Don't murder me...
(To Chorus:)

CHINA CAT SUNFLOWER

Words by ROBERT HUNTER
Music by JERRY GARCIA

*Play written fig. on 2nd verse.
**Chords implied by gtr. figures.

© 1969 ICE NINE PUBLISHING CO., INC.
This Arrangement © 1996 ICE NINE PUBLISHING CO., INC.
All Rights Reserved

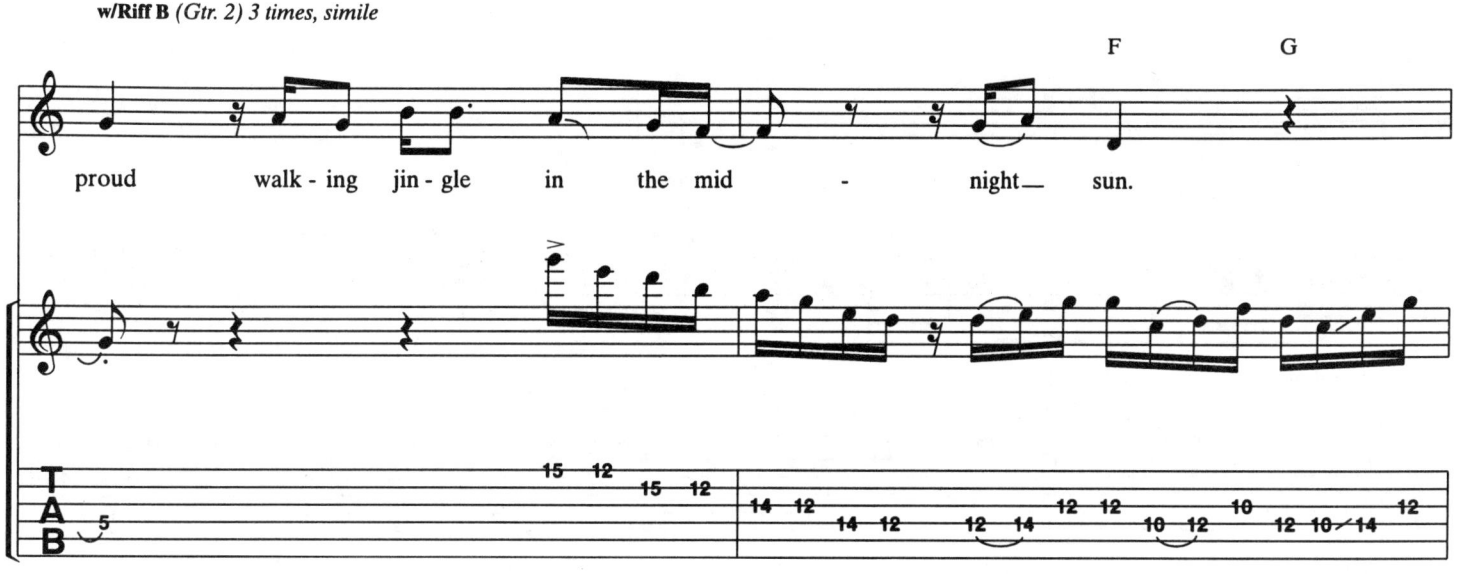

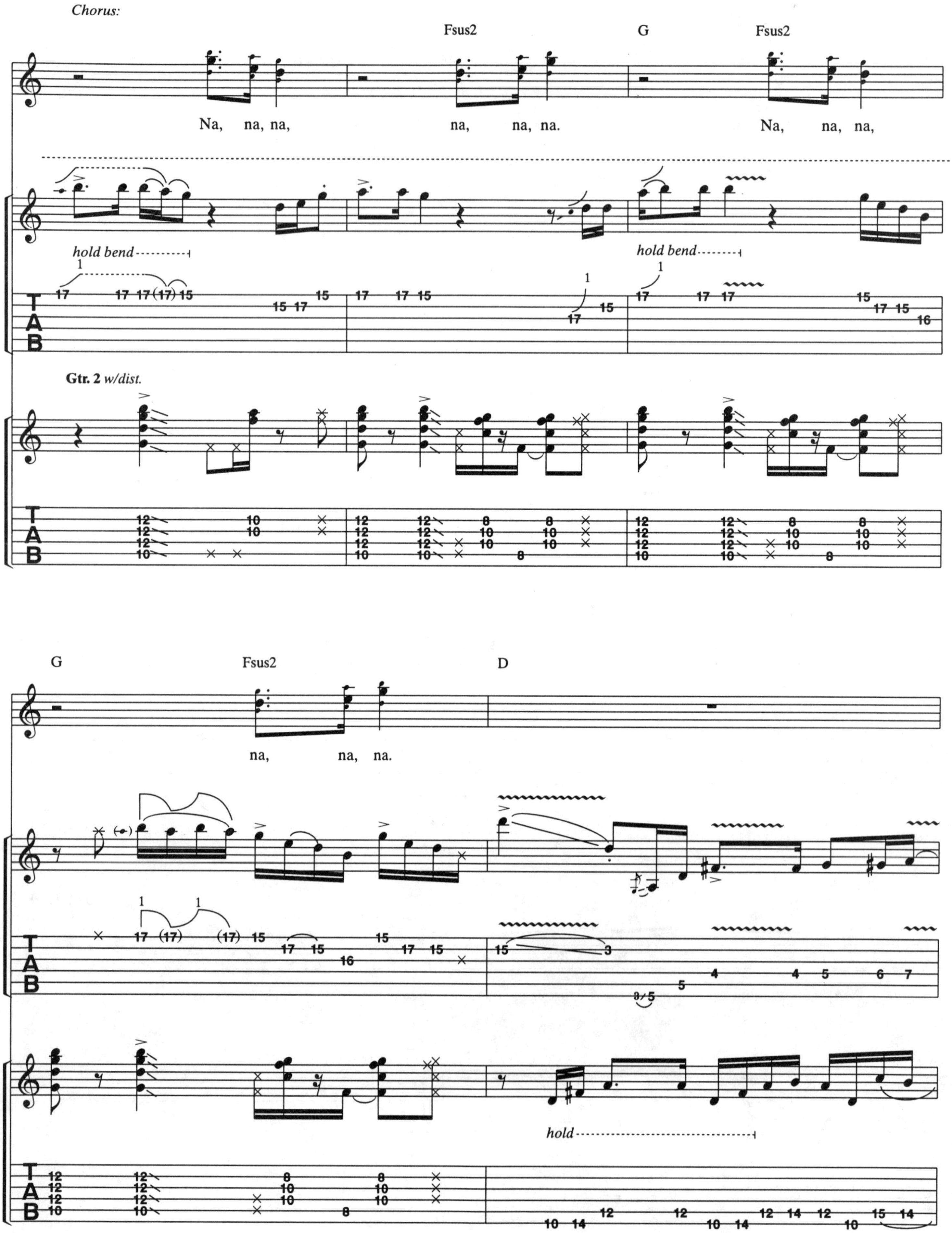
Chorus:
Fsus2
G
Fsus2
Na, na, na,
na, na, na.
Na, na, na,
hold bend
hold bend
Gtr. 2 w/dist.
G
Fsus2
D
na, na, na.
hold

31

32

Coda
G
Gsus2
G
Fsus2
Gtr. 1
hold bend
Gtr. 2
mf
G
Gsus2
G
Gsus2
grad. bend

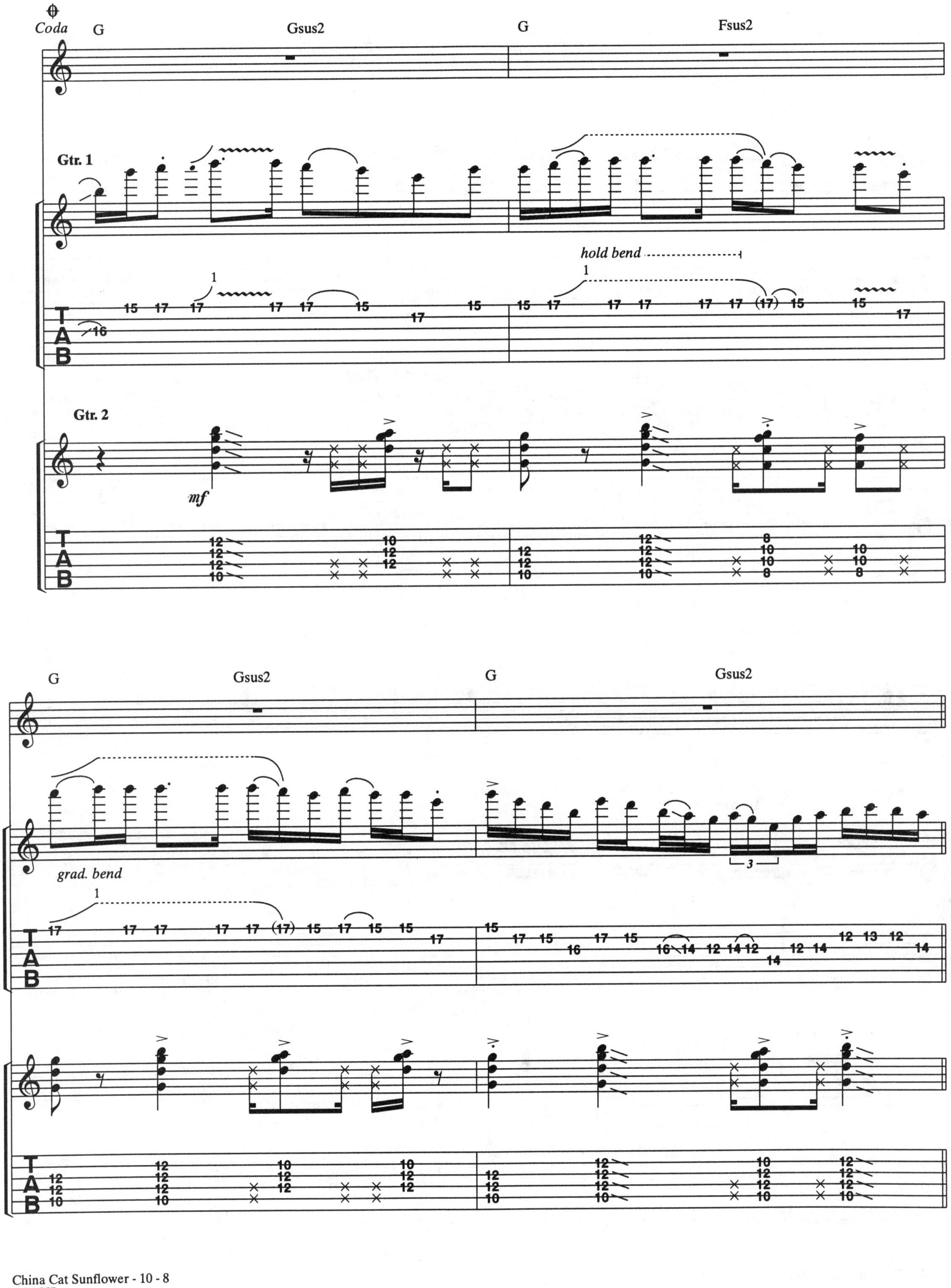

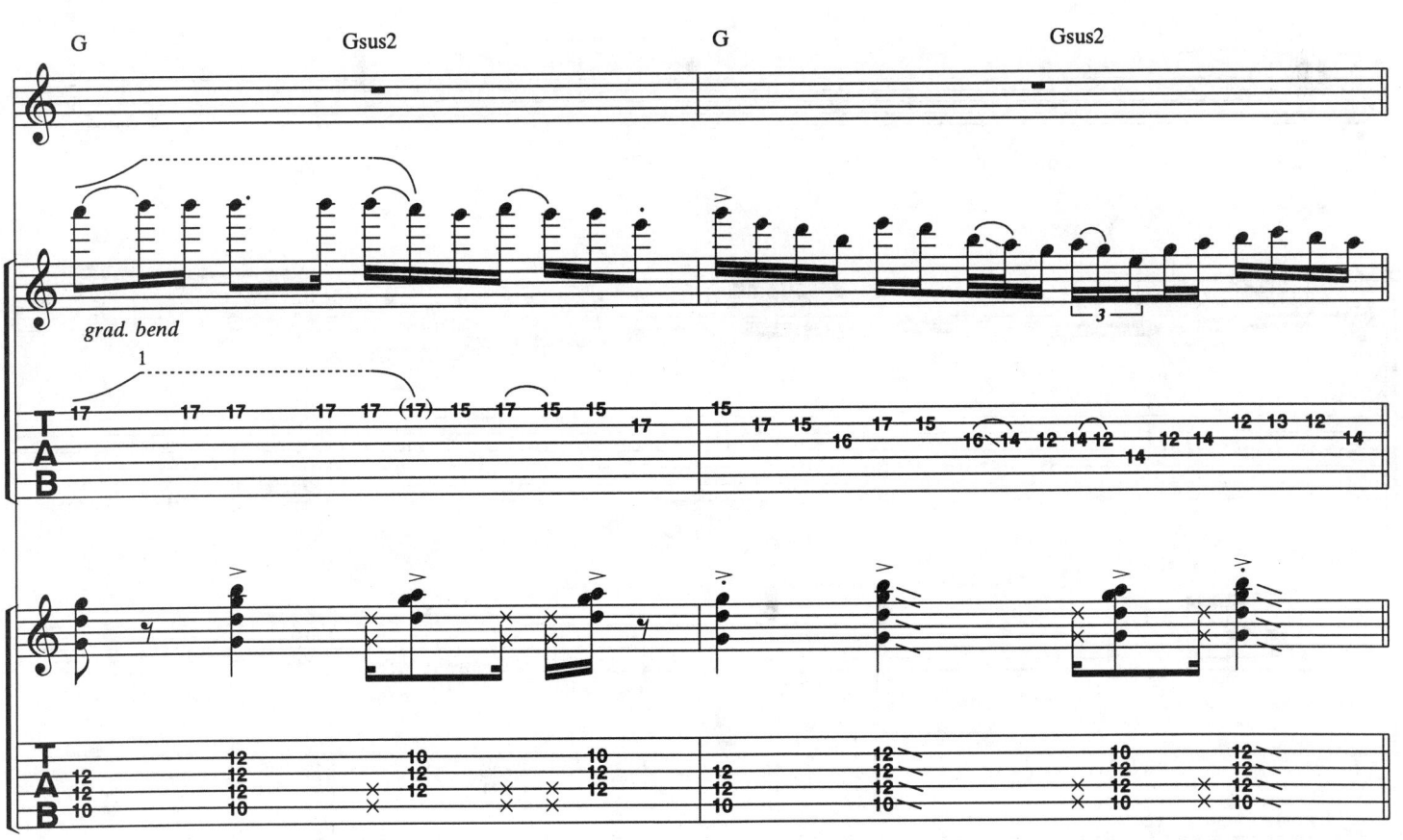

34

Outro:
D

Chi - na Cat,   Chi - na Cat,

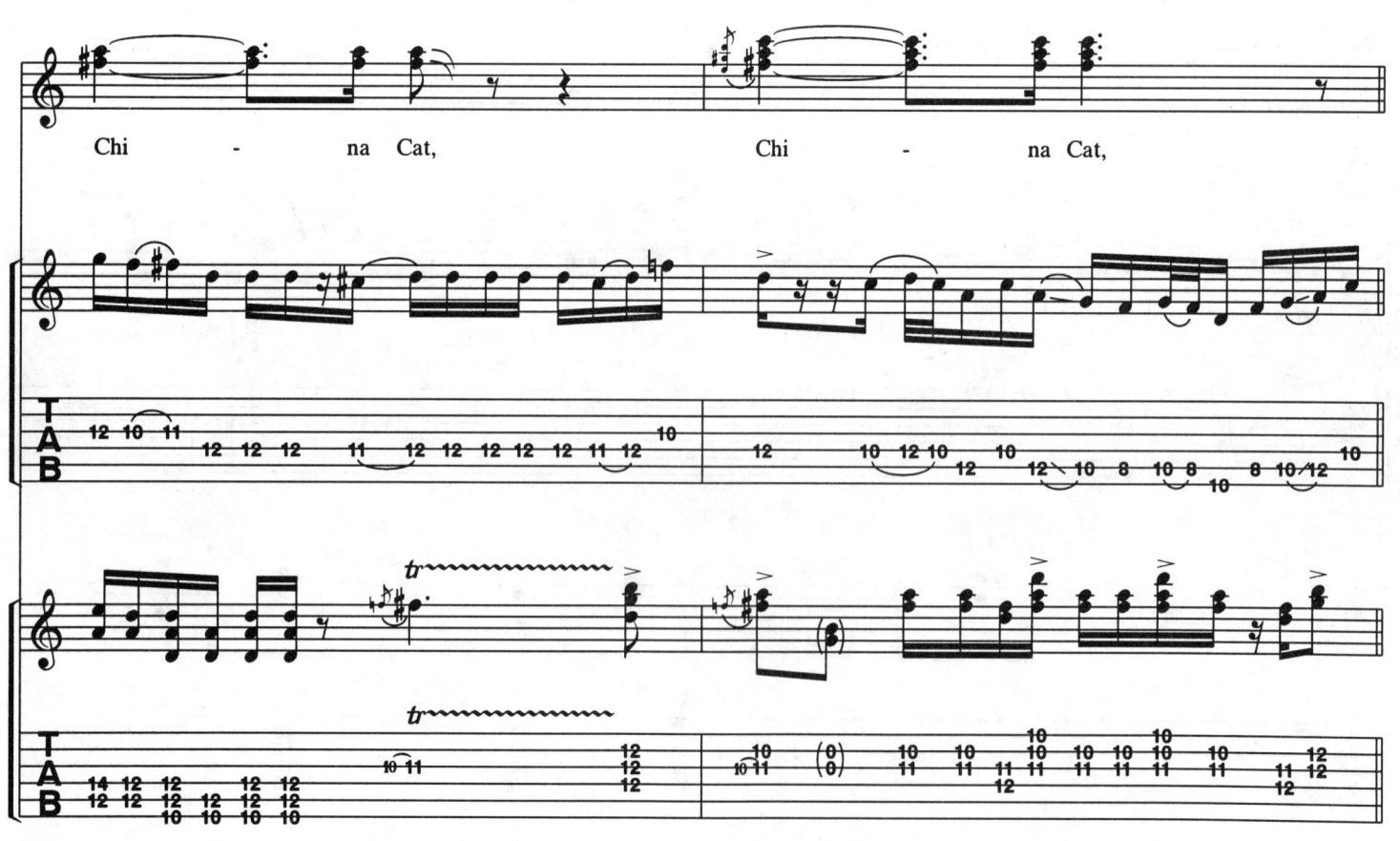

Chi - na Cat,   Chi - na Cat,

Verse 2:
Crazy cat, peekin' through a lace bandana
Like a one-eyed Cheshire,
Like a diamond-eye jack.
A leaf of all colors plays a golden string fiddle
To a double-e water fall over my back.
(To Chorus:)

Verse 3:
Comic book colors on a violin river,
Crying Leonardo words from out a silk trombone.
I rang a silent bell beneath a shower of pearls
In the eagle winged palace of the Queen Chinee.
(To Coda)

I KNOW YOU RIDER

Trad., Arrangement by
GRATEFUL DEAD

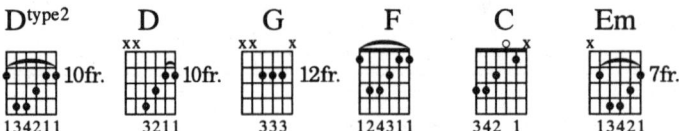

Moderate country feel in 2 ♩ = 90

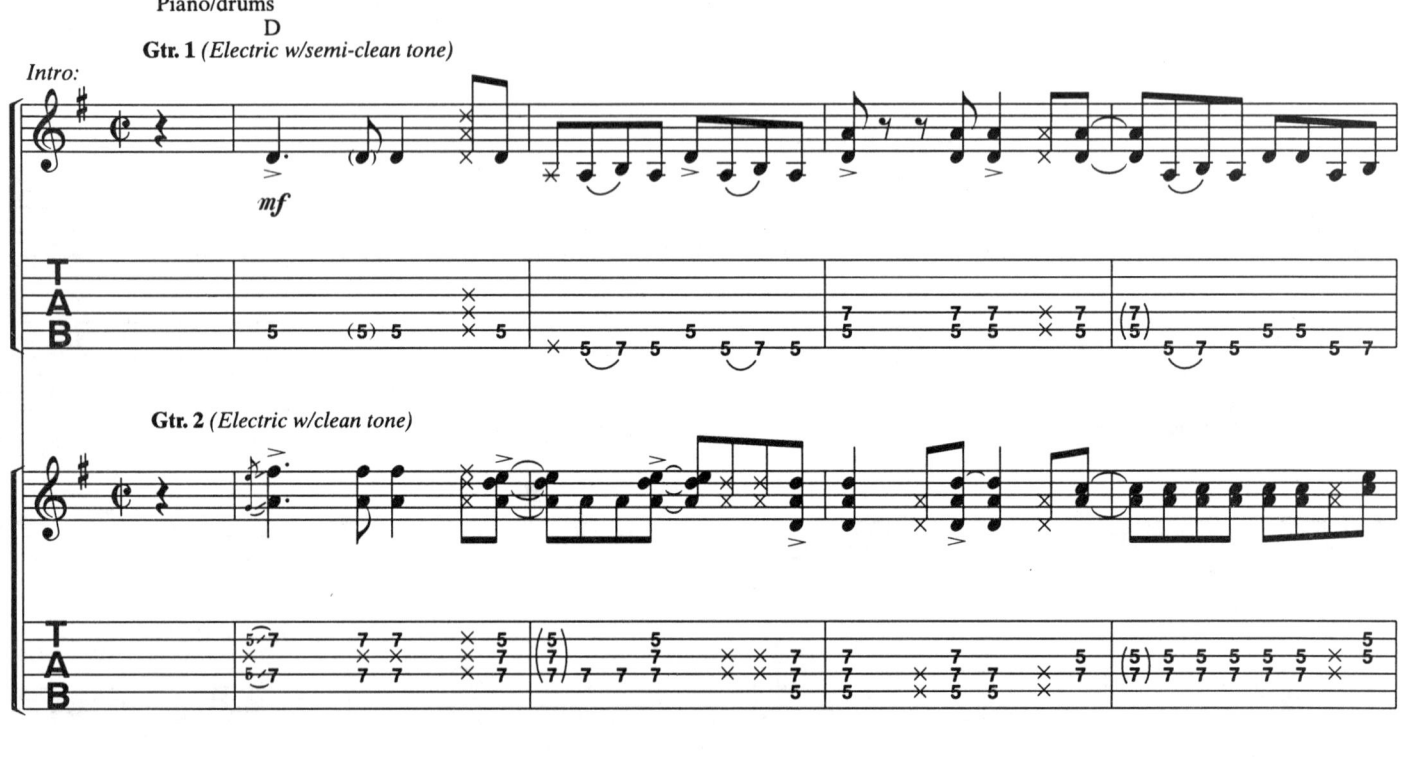

I Know You Rider - 12 - 1
PG9557

© 1972 ICE NINE PUBLISHING CO., INC.
This Arrangement © 1996 ICE NINE PUBLISHING CO., INC.
All Rights Reserved

41

I Know You Rider - 12 - 2
PG9557

46

I Know You Rider - 12 - 7
PG9557

48

50

I Know You Rider - 12 - 11
PG9557

ME AND MY UNCLE

Words and Music by
JOHN PHILLIPS

Verses:
Em
G
1. (A) me and my un - cle
2.-5. See additional lyrics
(a) went rid - ing down
mp
1/2
Rhy. Fig. 1
hold
hold
Em
to south Col - o - rad -
1/4
1/4
end Rhy. Fig. 1

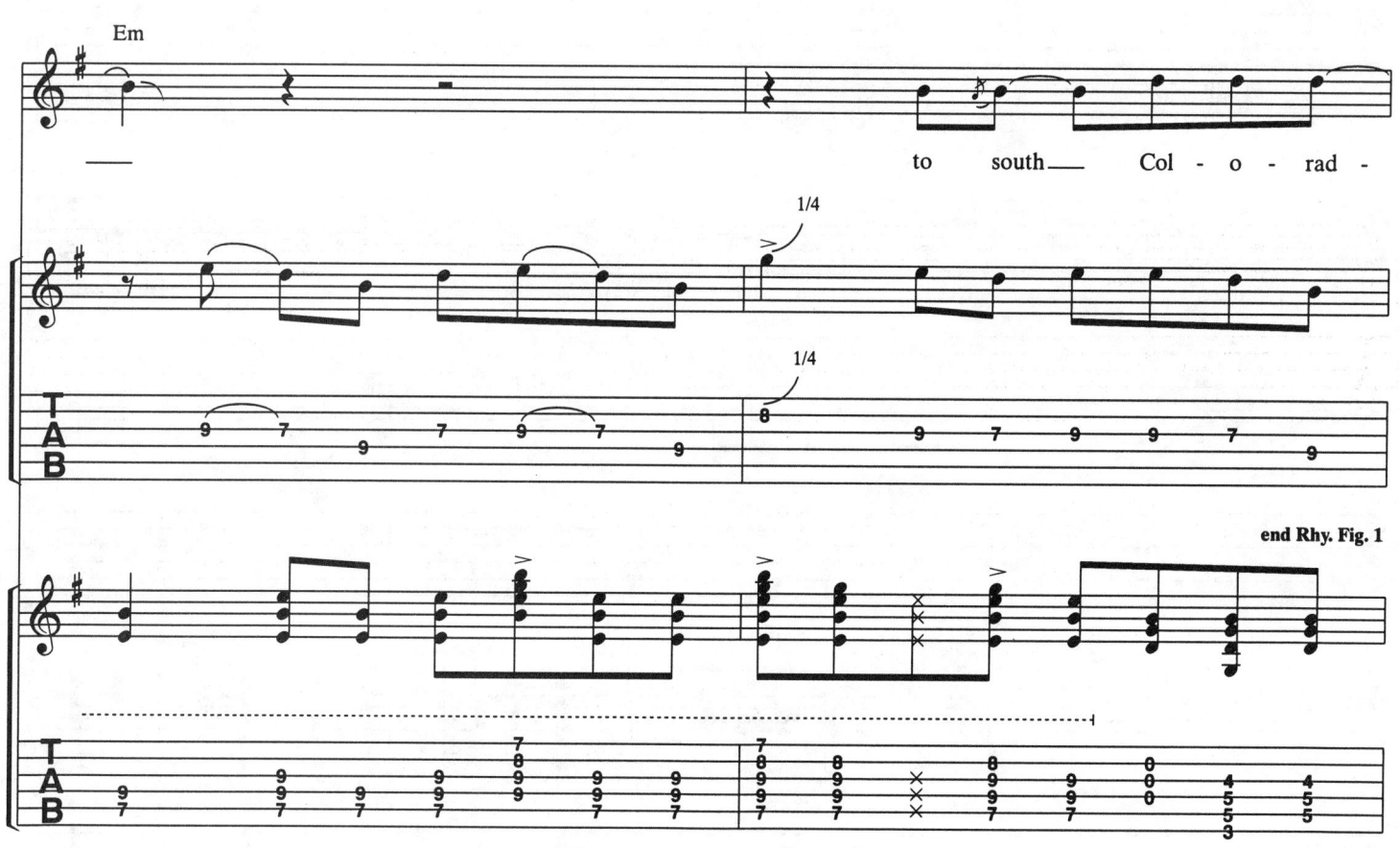

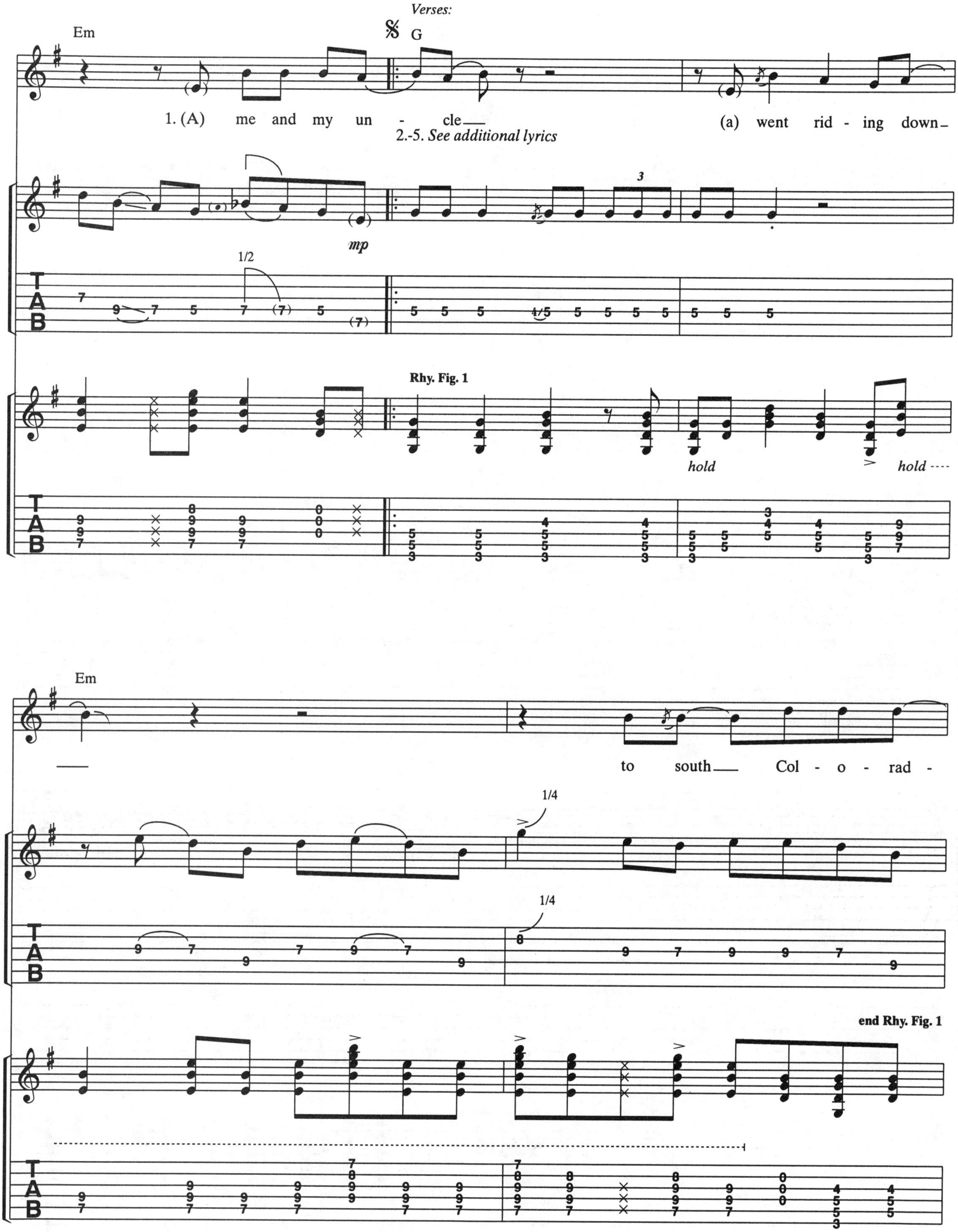

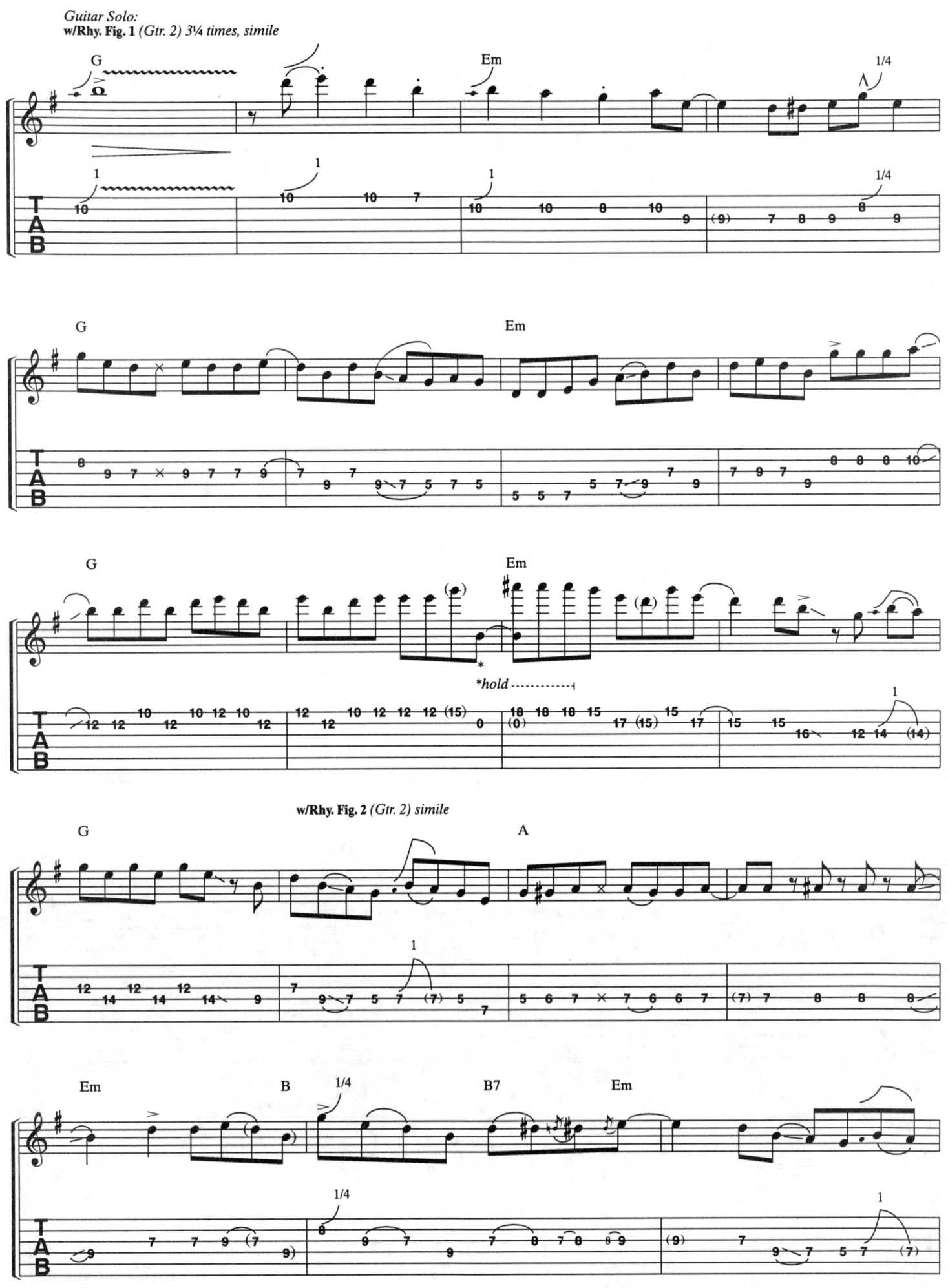

Me And My Uncle - 8 - 5
PG9557

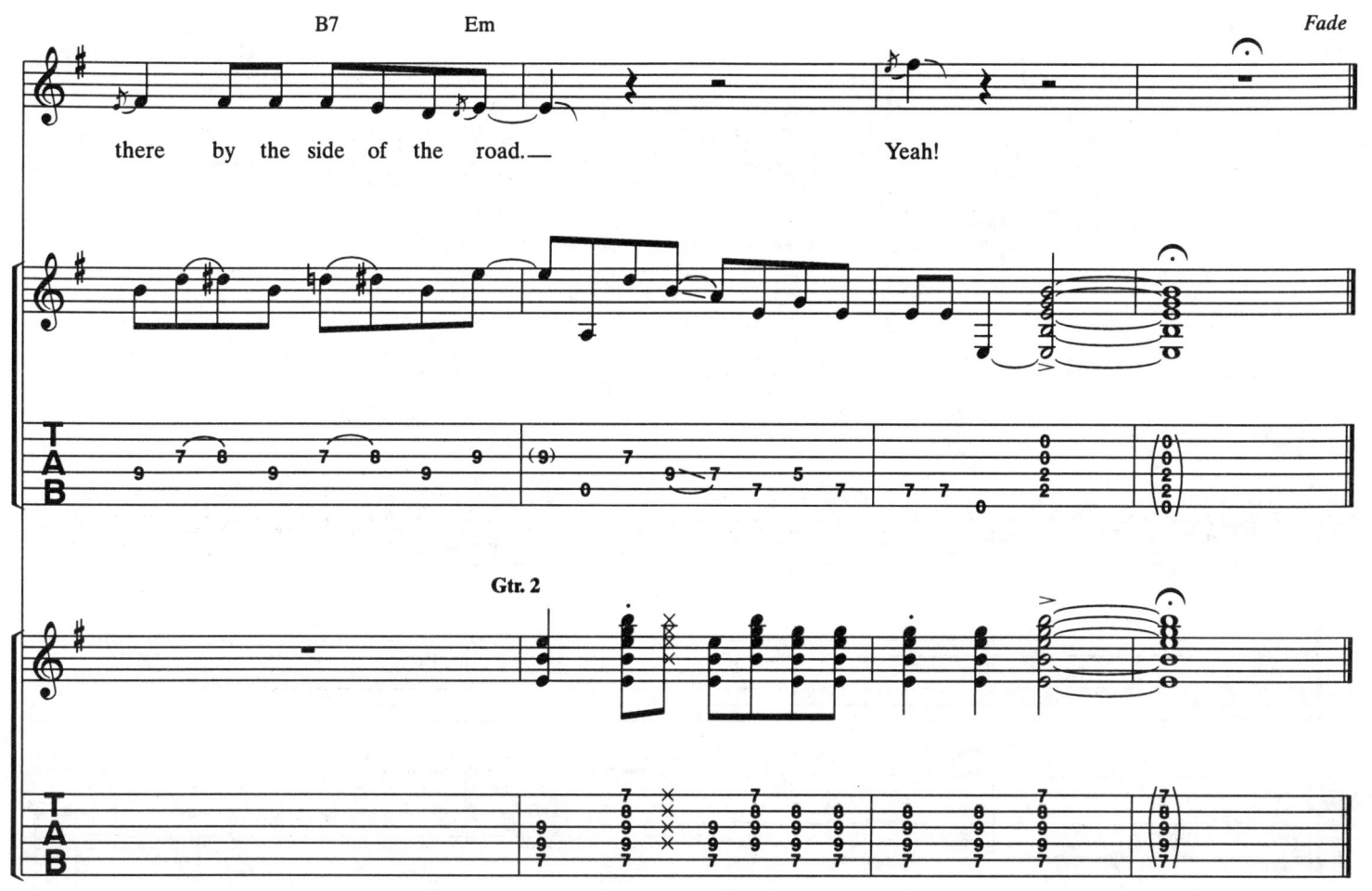

Verse 2:
And I took the horses up to the stall.
Went to the barroom, ordered drinks for all.
Three days in the saddle; you know my body hurt.
It being summer, I took off my shirt
And I tried to wash off some of that dusty dirt.

Verse 3:
West Texas cowboys, they's all around.
With liqueur and money they loaded down.
So soon after payday, 'know it seemed a shame.
You know my uncle, he starts a friendly game,
Yeah, of high-low Jack and the winner take the hand.

Verse 4:
My uncle starts winning, cowboys got sore.
One of them called him, and then two more.
Accused him of cheating, whoa, no it couldn't be.
I know my uncle, he's as honest as me.
Hey, now, I'm as honest as a desperate man can be.

Verse 5:
One of them cowboys, he starts to draw,
And I shot him down Lord; he never saw.
Shot me another; that man, he won't grow old.
In the confusion my uncle grabbed the gold,
Hey, and we high-tailed it down to Mexico.

GOING DOWN THE ROAD FEELIN' BAD

Trad., Arrangement by
GRATEFUL DEAD

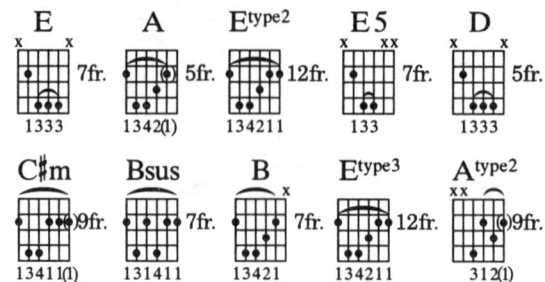

Going Down The Road Feelin' Bad - 11 - 3
PG9557

70

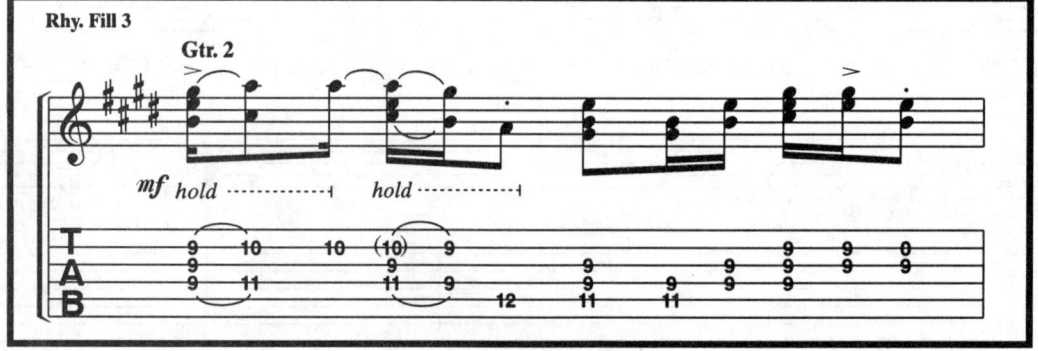

Verse 2:
My love's bigger than a Cadillac;
I tried to show you but you drive me bad.
Your love for me has got to be real;
You gonna know just how I feel.
Love's a real and not fade away.
Not fade away.

Verse 2:
Goin' where the water tastes like wine.
Well, I'm goin' where the water tastes like wine.
Goin' where the water tastes like wine.
I don't wanna be treated this old way.

ONE MORE SATURDAY NIGHT

Words and Music by
BOB WEIR

Moderately fast blues ♩ = 166

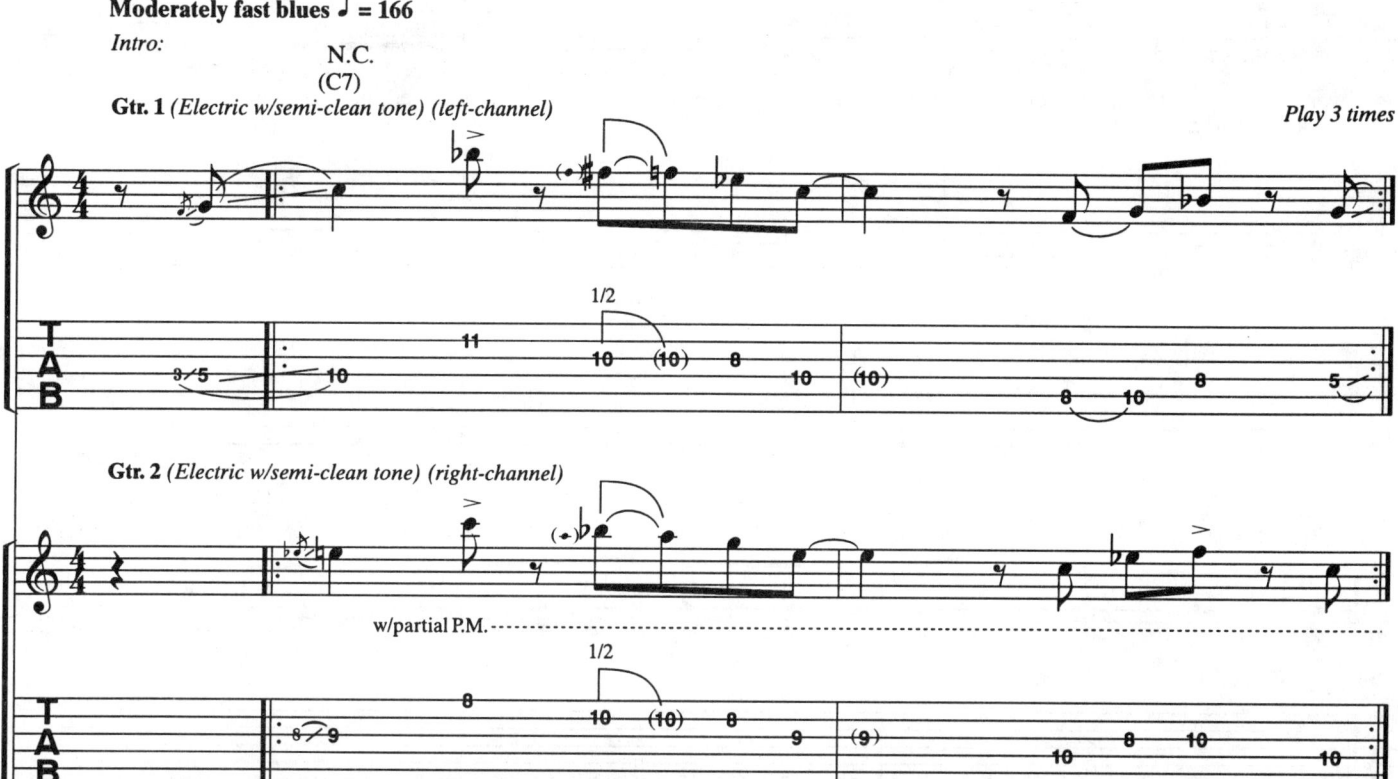

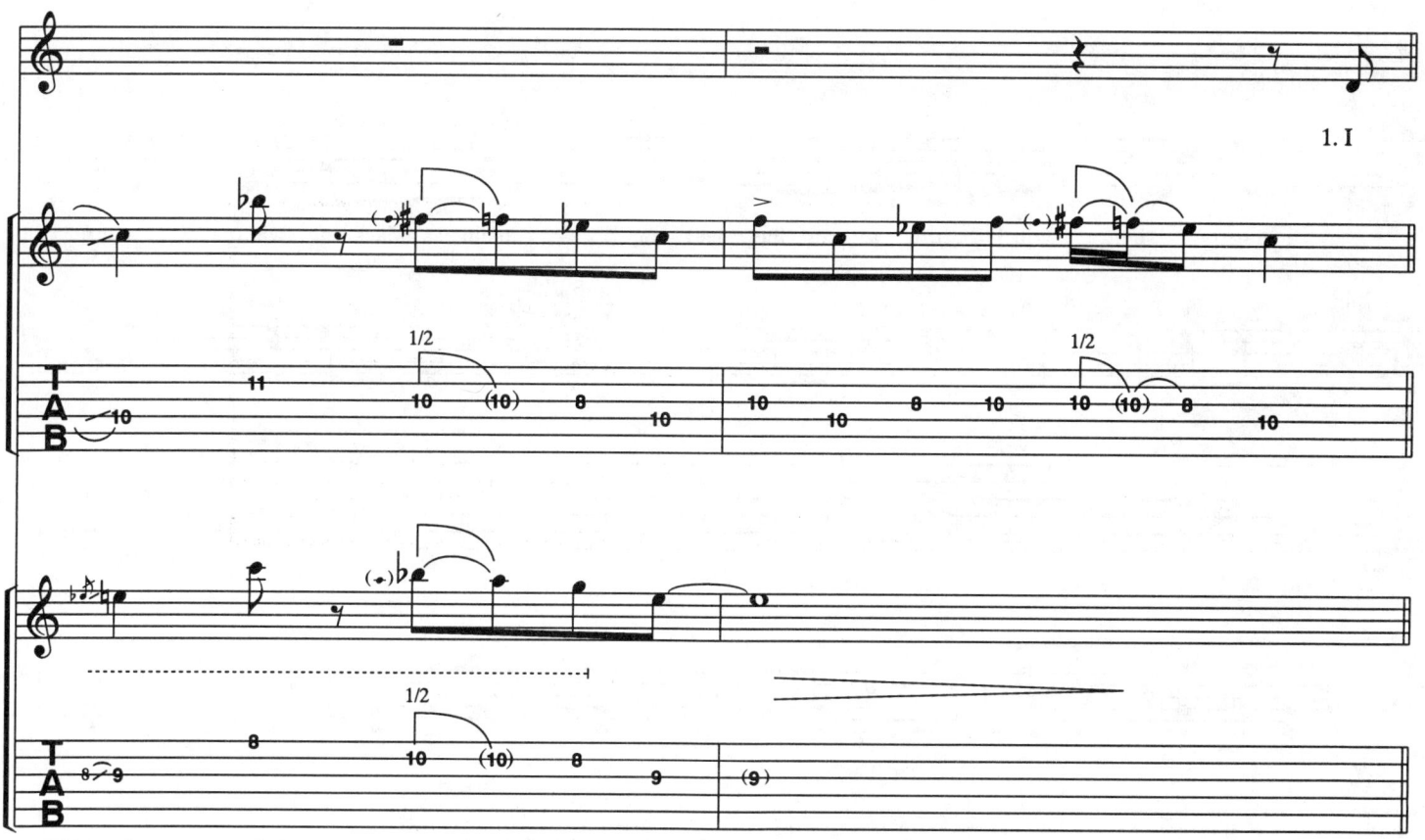

One More Saturday Night - 13 - 1
PG9557

© 1972 ICE NINE PUBLISHING CO., INC.
This Arrangement © 1996 ICE NINE PUBLISHING CO., INC.
All Rights Reserved

72

*Basic harmony.

One More Saturday Night - 13 - 2
PG9557

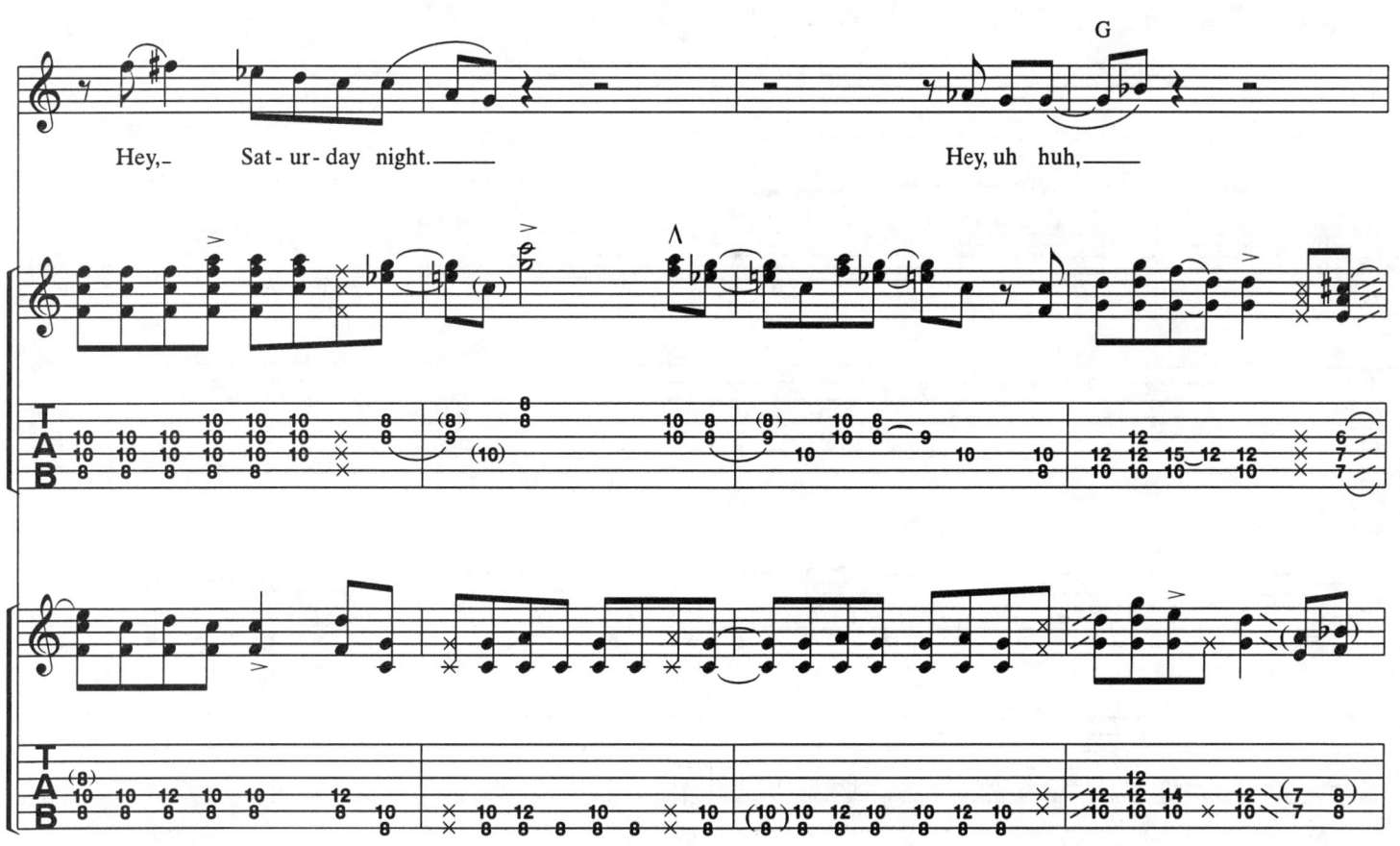

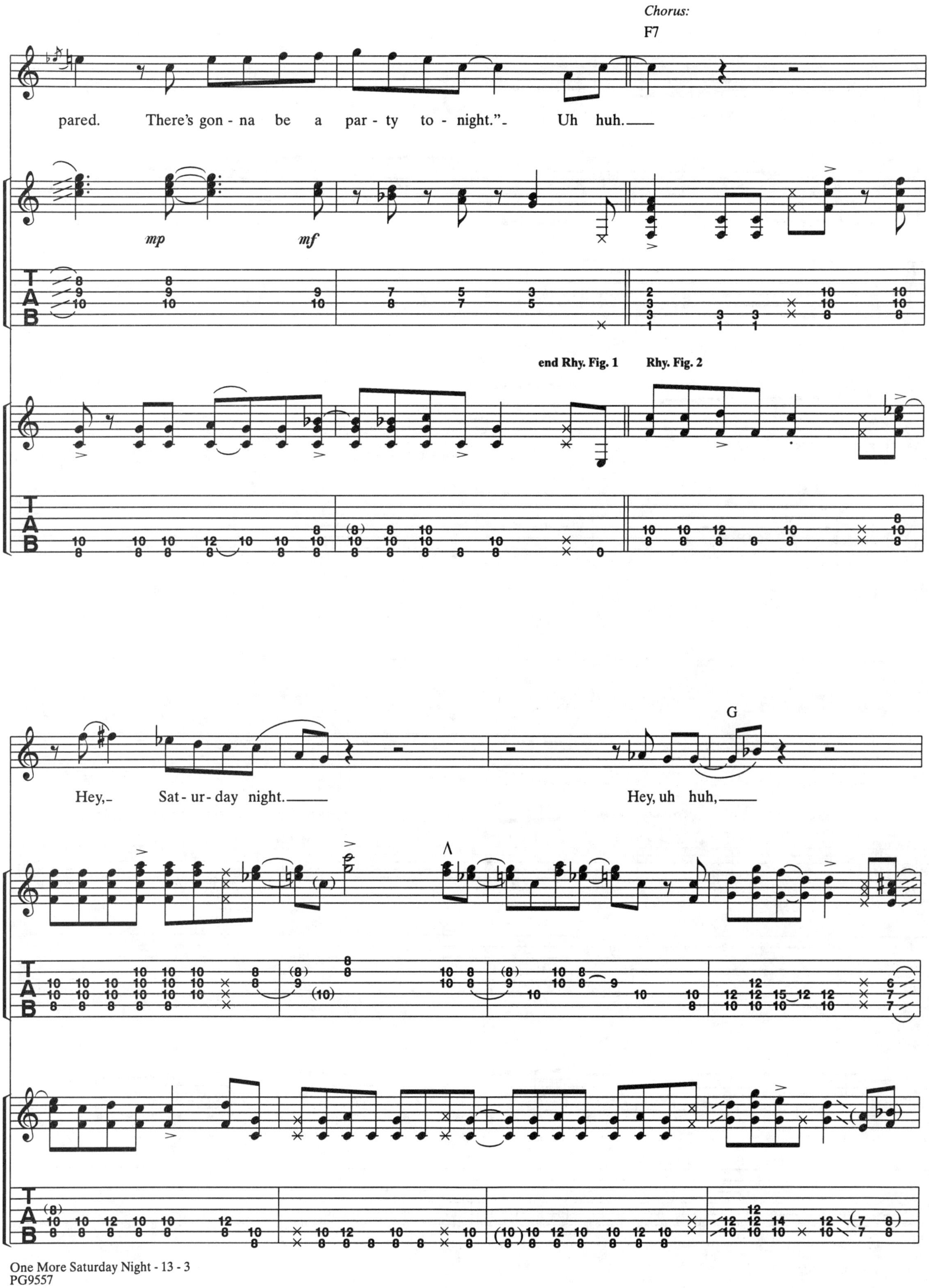
Chorus:
F7
pared. There's gon - na be a par - ty to - night." Uh huh.
mp
mf
end Rhy. Fig. 1
Rhy. Fig. 2
G
Hey, Sat - ur - day night.
Hey, uh huh,

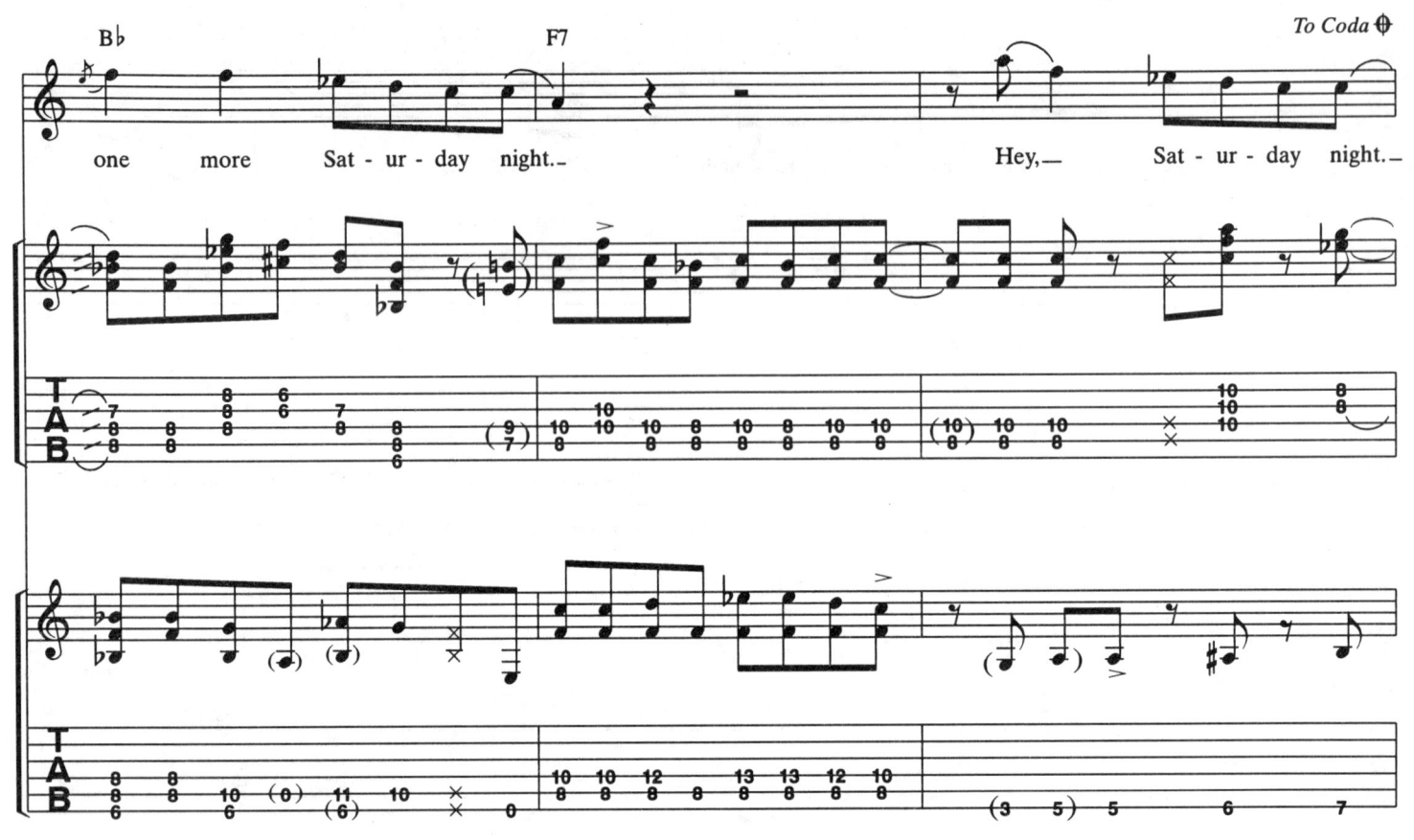

Coda
C7
Gtr. 1
hold
N.C.
(C7)
1/2
1/2

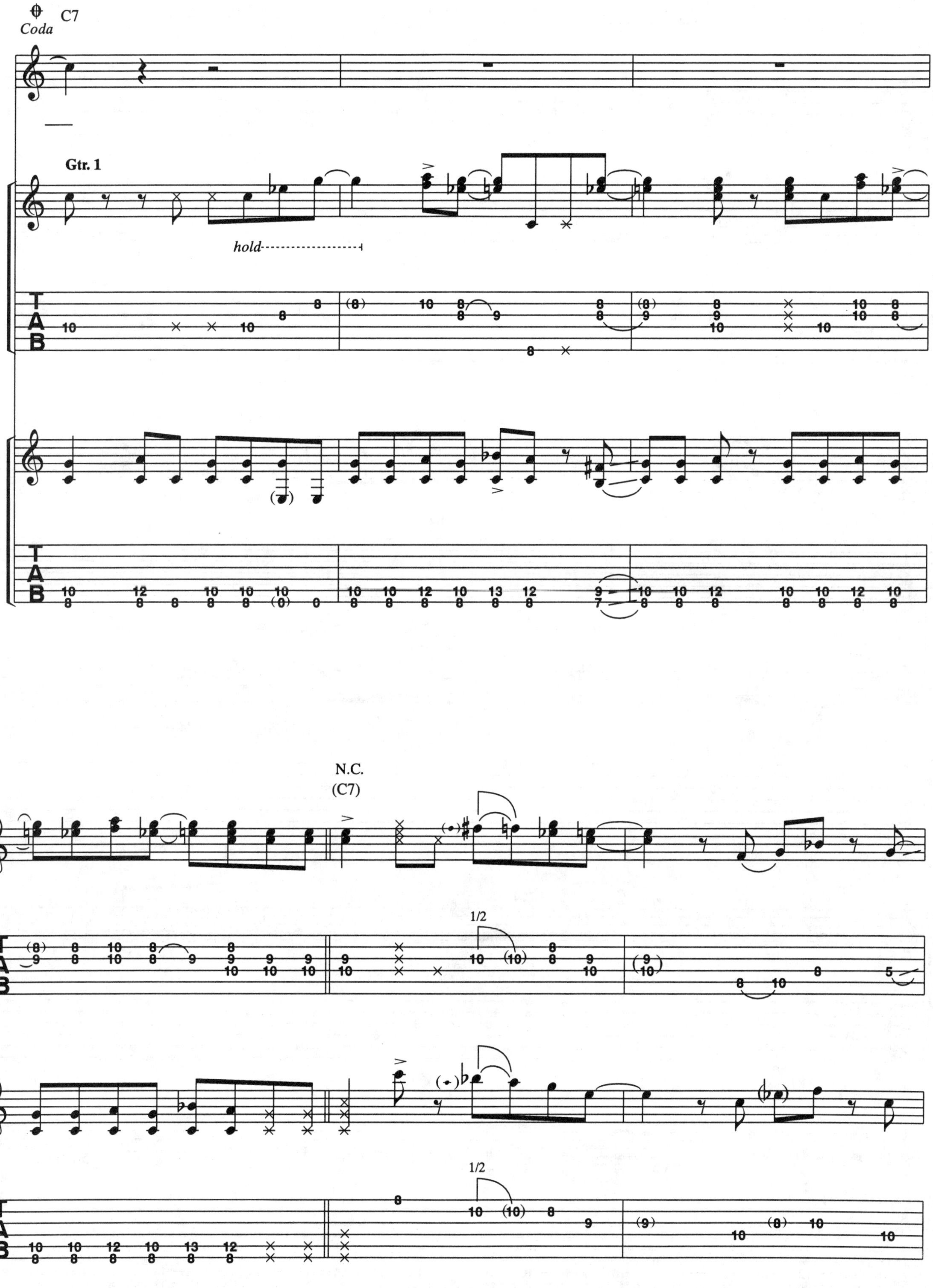

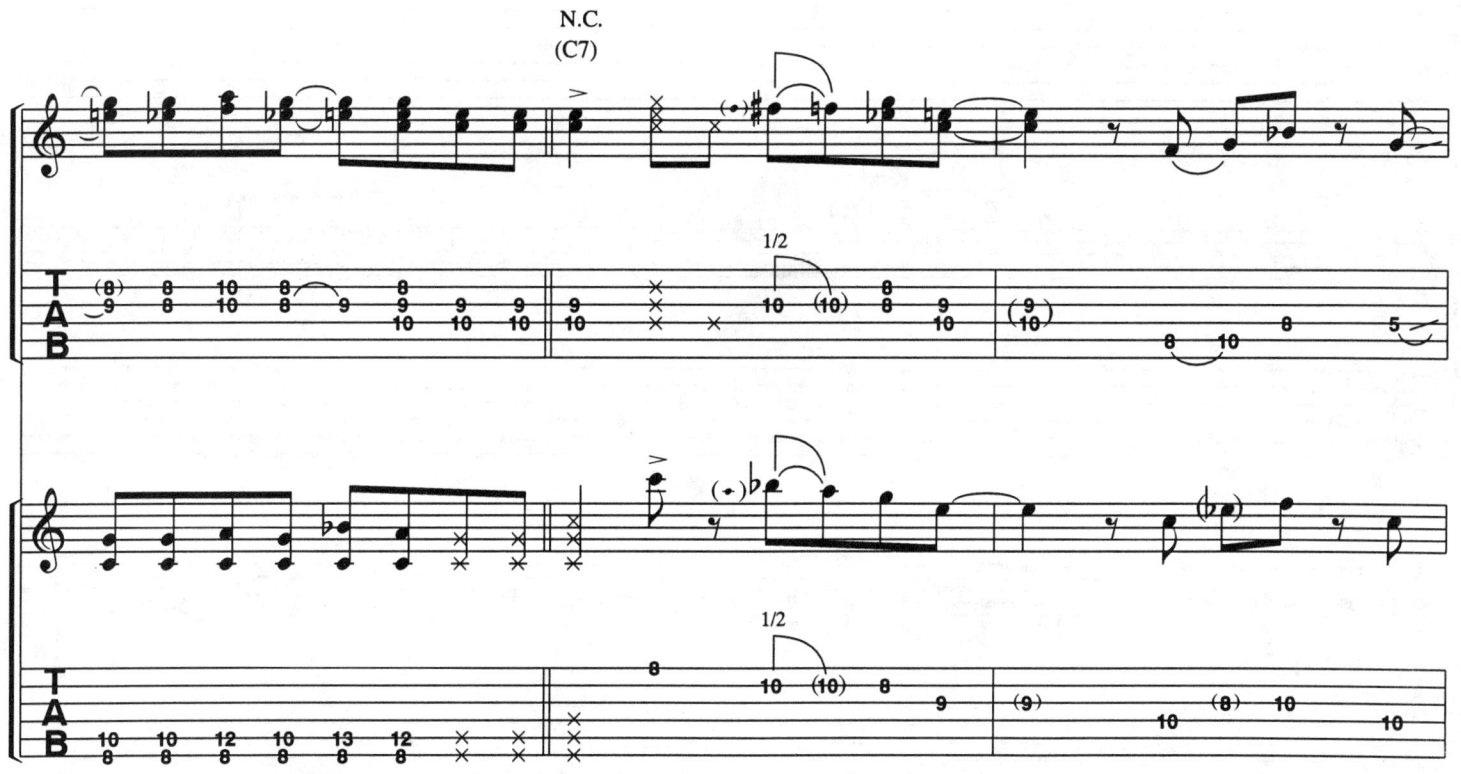

G5 G♯5 A5 A♯5 B5
hold
Outro:
C7
Hey, an - oth - er Sat - ur - day night.
Hey, an - oth - er Sat - ur - day night.
Bkgd vcl: One more Sat - ur - day night. One

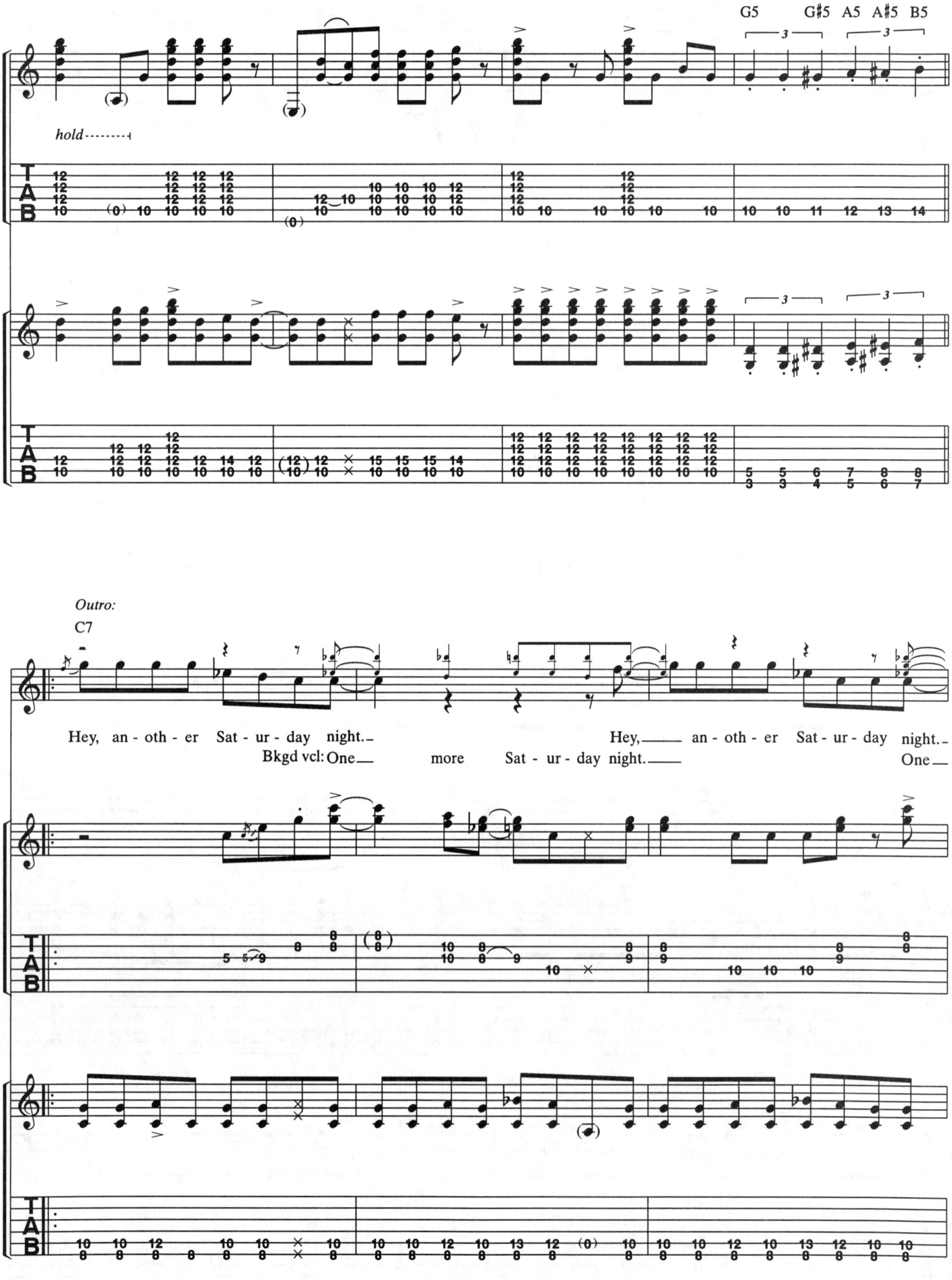

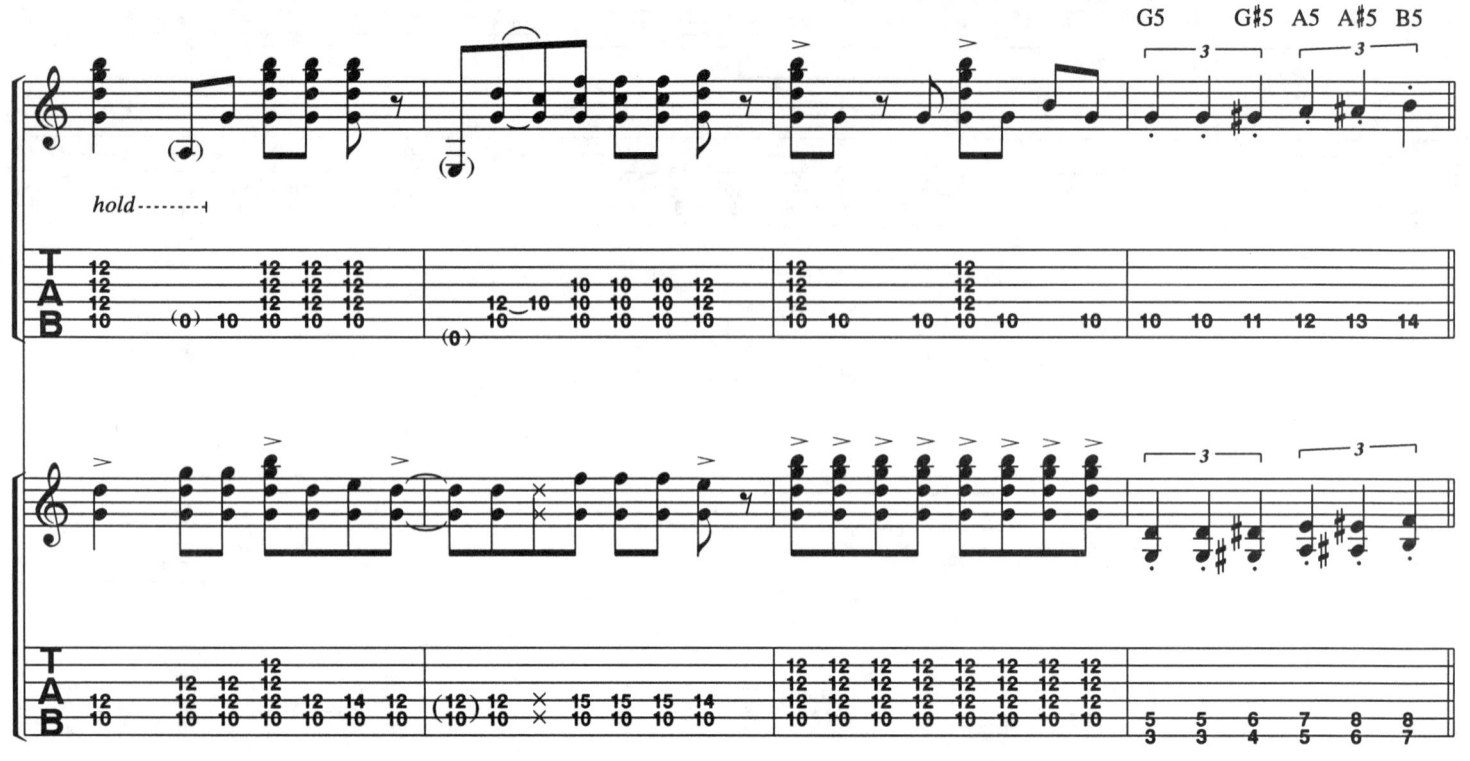

81

*Play as sub. on 1st repeat only - Gtrs.1 and 2.

Lyrics: more Saturday night. Ev-'ry-bod-y get by. (Bkgd vcl. simile)

Hey, an-oth-er Sat-ur-day night.

One More Saturday Night - 13 - 11
PG9557

82

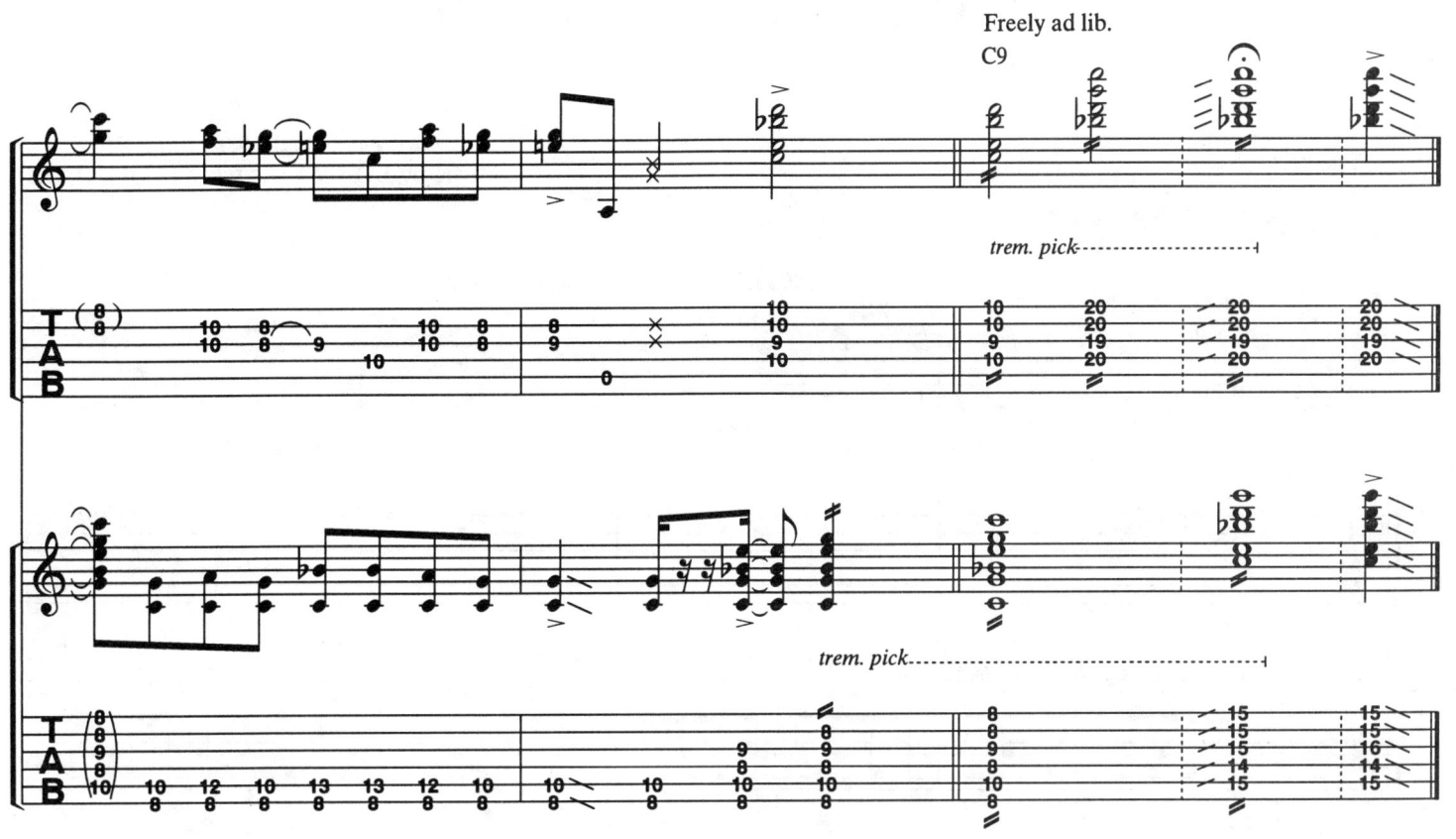

Verse 2:
Everybody's dancing at the local armory,
With a basement full of dynamite and live artillery.
Temperature keeps risin'; everybody gettin' high.
Come the rockin' stroke of midnight, the whole place is gonna fly.
(To Chorus:)

Verse 3:
I turn on Channel Six; the President comes on the news.
Says, "I get no satisfaction, that's why I sing the blues."
His wife says, "Don't get crazy, Lord, you know what to do.
Just crank that old Victrola, put on your rockin' shoes."
(To Chorus:)

Verse 4:
Then God way up in heaven, for whatever it was worth,
Thought He'd have a big ol' party; thought He'd call it planet earh.
Don't worry about tomorrow, Lord, you'll know it when it comes,
When the rockin', rollin' music meets the risin', shinin' sun.
(To Chorus:)

PLAYING IN THE BAND

Words by ROBERT HUNTER
Music by BOB WEIR and MICKEY HART

Moderately fast ♩ = 122
Intro:

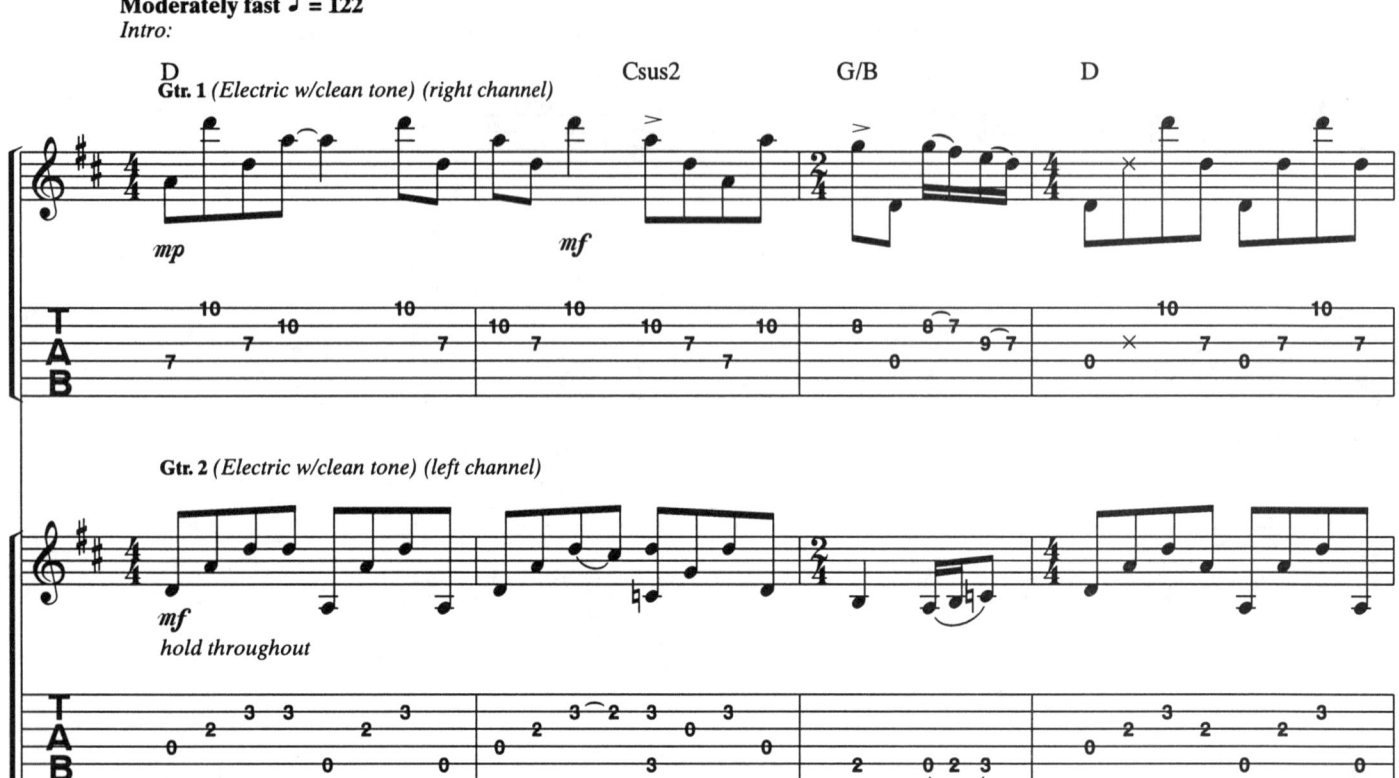

Playing in the Band - 7 - 1
PG9557

© 1971 ICE NINE PUBLISHING CO., INC.
This Arrangement © 1996 ICE NINE PUBLISHING CO., INC.
All Rights Reserved

85

Playing in the Band - 7 - 2
PG9557

87

Playing in the Band - 7 - 4
PG9557

Verse 2:
Some folks look answers,
Others look for fights.
Some folks up in tree-tops,
Just to look to see the sights.
Oh, I can tell your future;
Whoa, just look what's in your hand.
But I can't stop for nothin',
I'm just playing in the band.
(To Chorus:)

Verse 3:
Standin' on a tower, world at my command,
You just keep a turnin' while I'm playin' in the band.
If a man among you got no sin upon his hand,
Women cast a stone at me for playing in the band.

ST. STEPHEN

Words by ROBERT HUNTER
Music by JERRY GARCIA and PHIL LESH

Moderately slow ♩ = 64
Freely

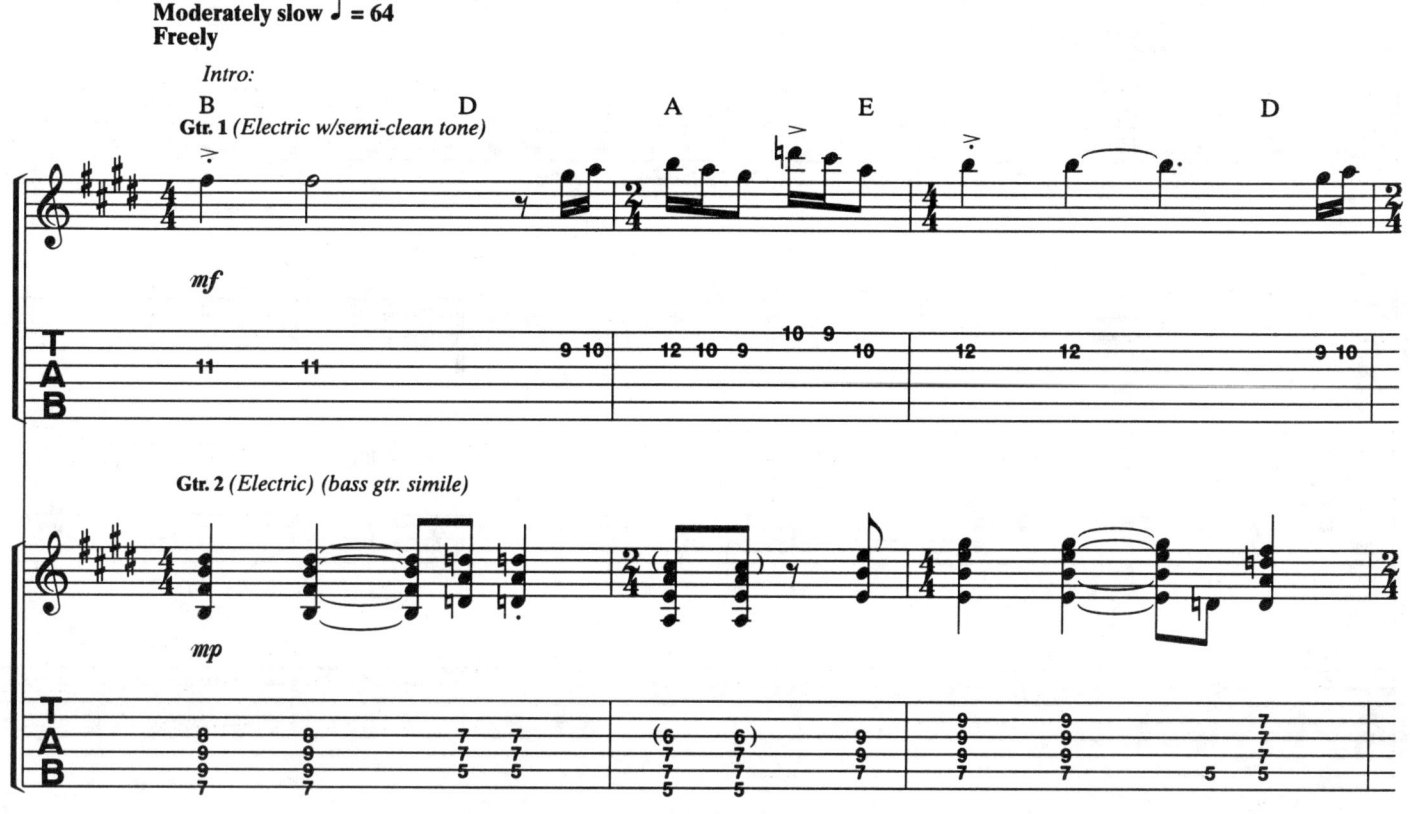

94

St. Stephen - 15 - 4
PG9557

98

St. Stephen - 15 - 8
PG9557

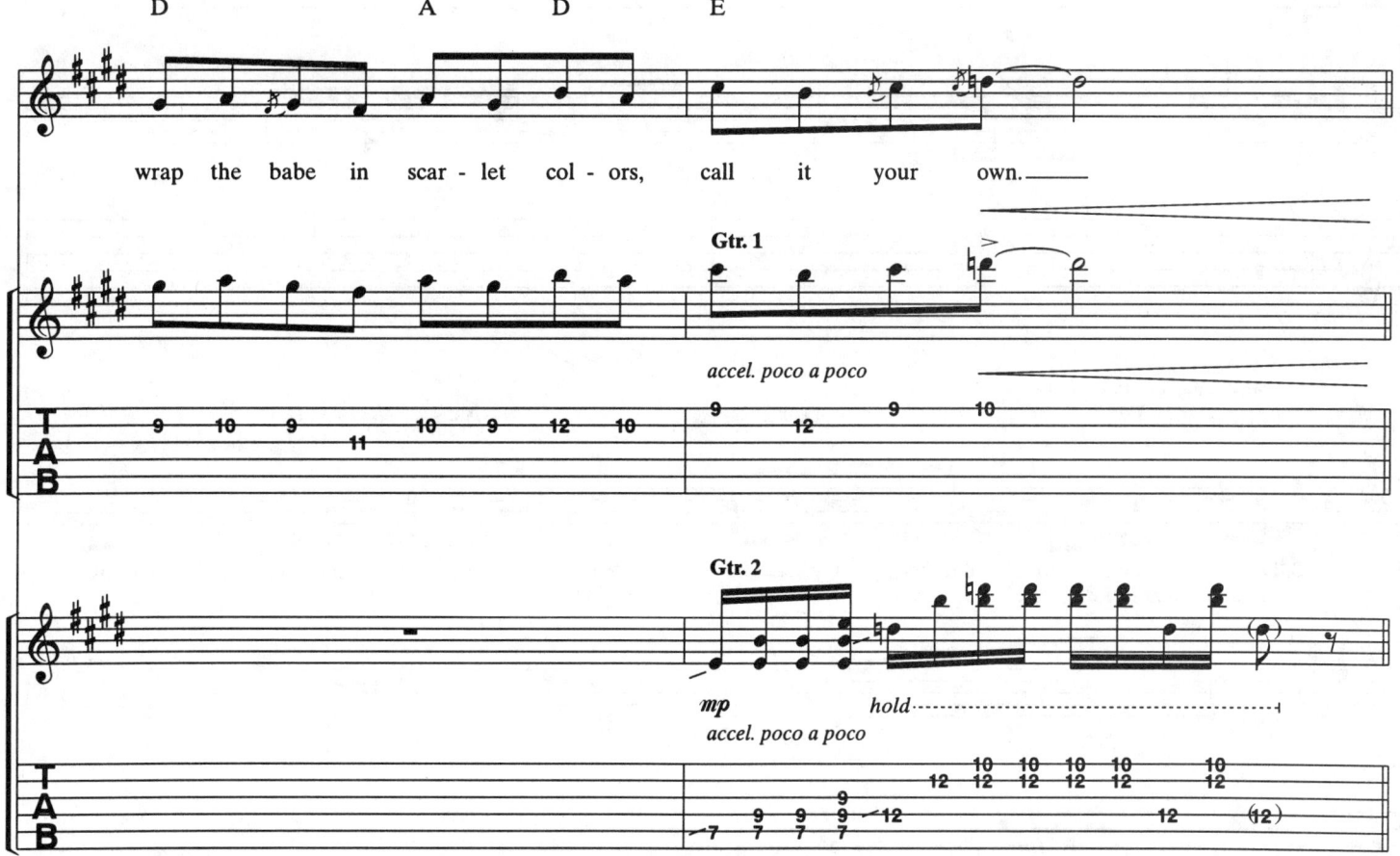

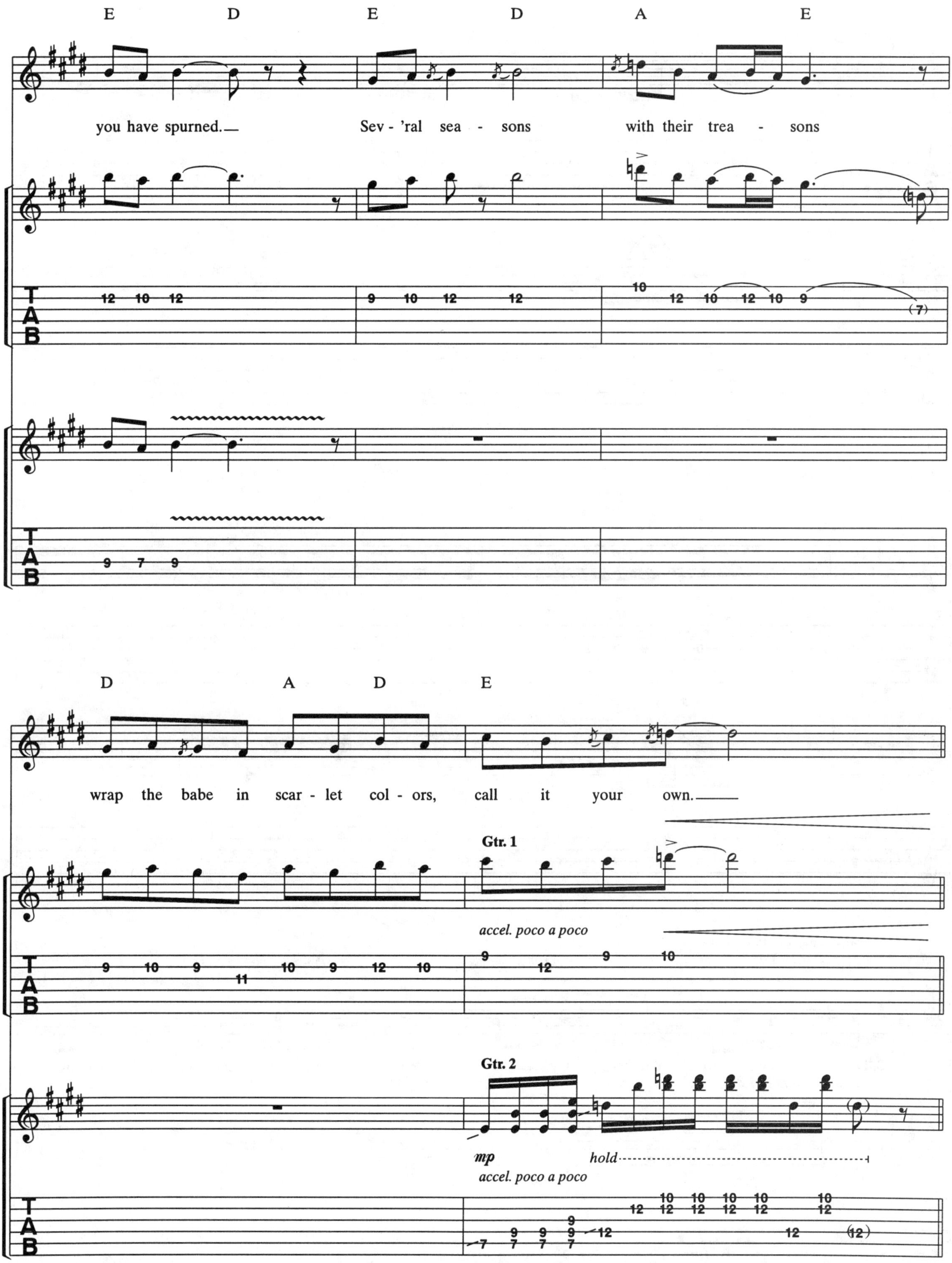
E D E D A E
you have spurned.__ Sev - 'ral sea - sons with their trea - sons
D A D E
wrap the babe in scar - let col - ors, call it your own.___
Gtr. 1
accel. poco a poco
Gtr. 2
mp
hold
accel. poco a poco

3. Did he doubt or did he try? Answers a-plenty in the by-and-by.
4. *See additional lyrics*

102

St. Stephen - 15 - 12
PG9557

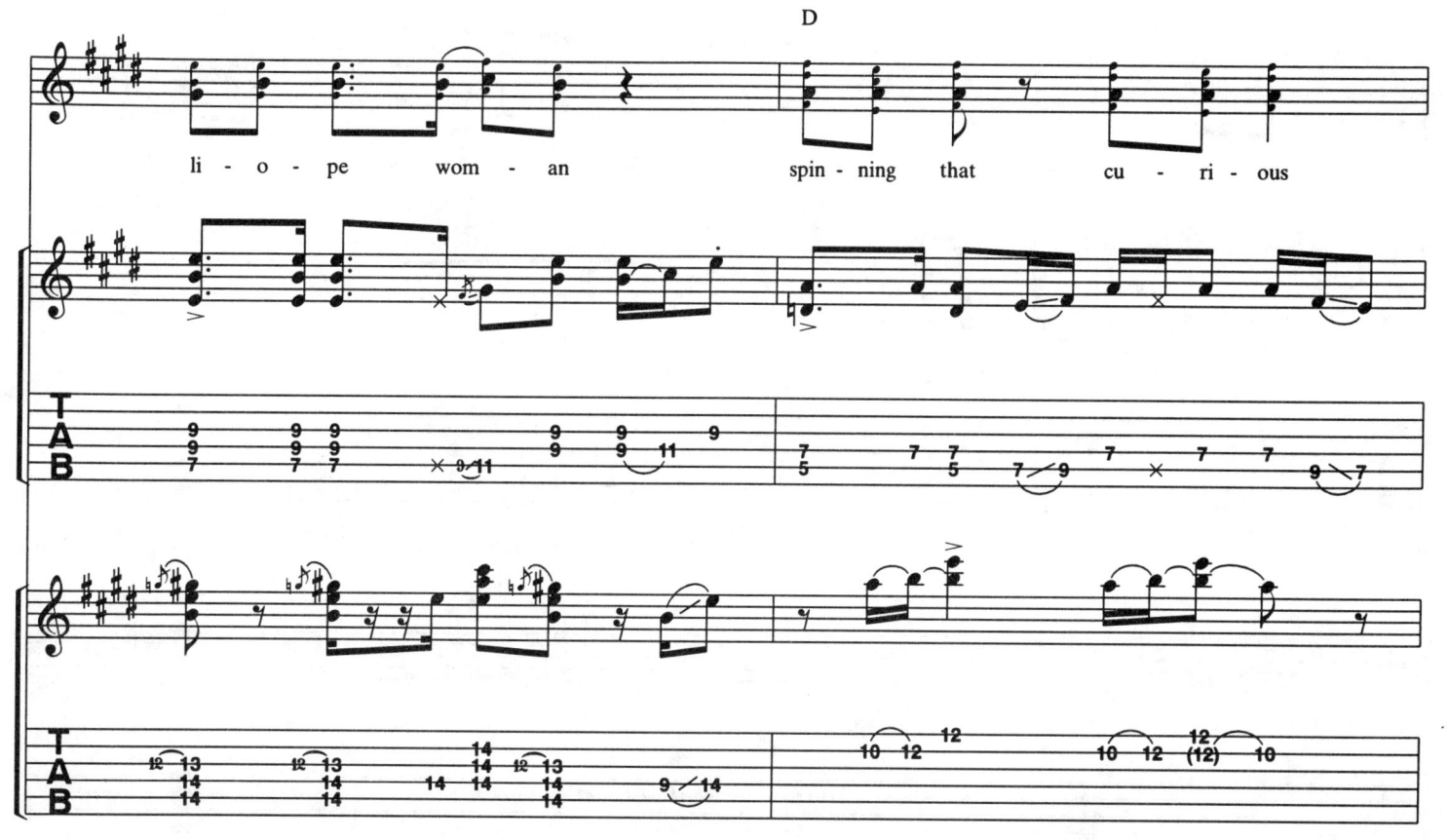

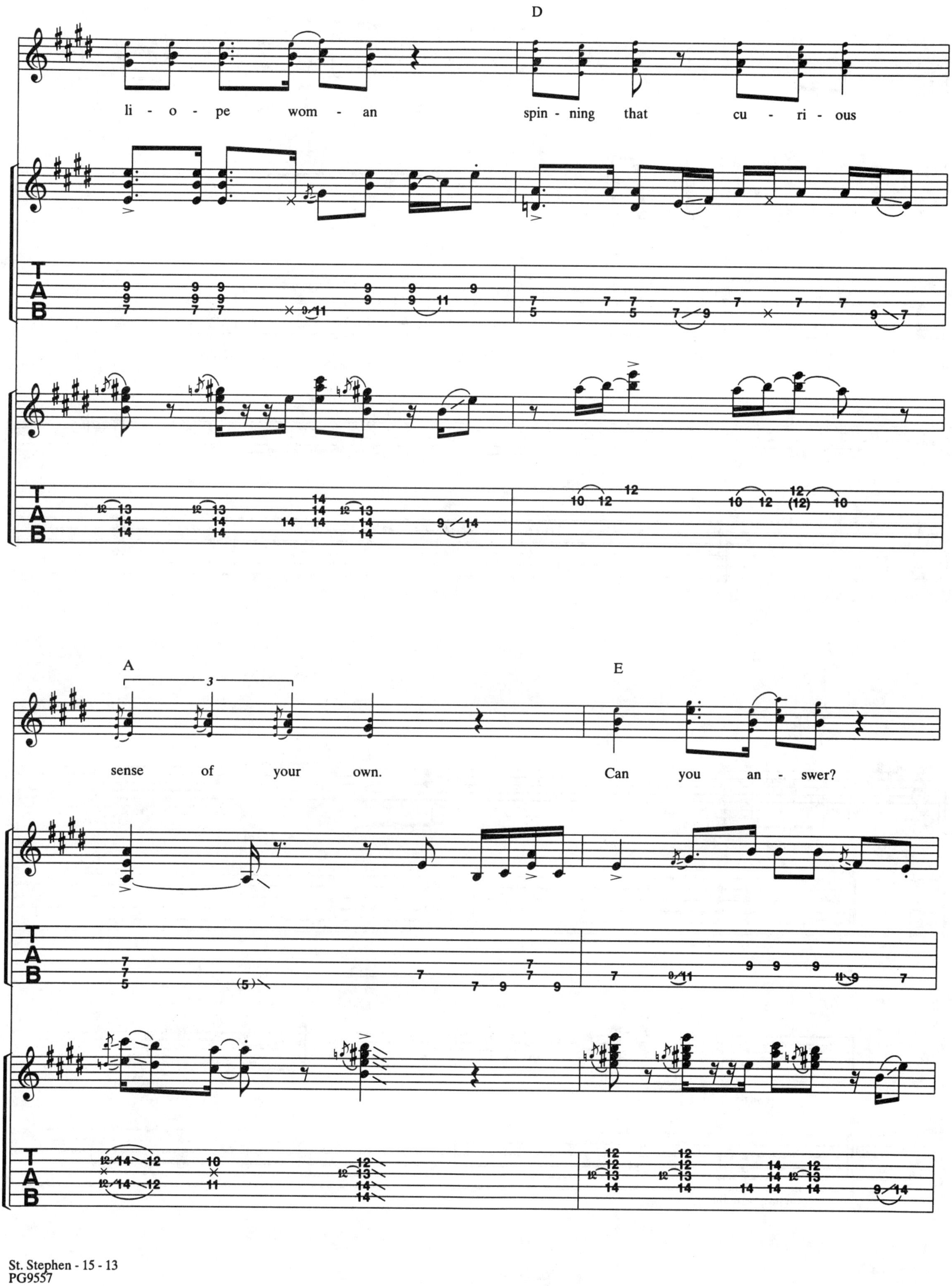
D
li - o - pe wom - an spin - ning that cu - ri - ous
A
E
sense of your own. Can you an - swer?

104

*Vamp progression in E.

St. Stephen - 15 - 14
PG9557

105

Verse 4:
Saint Stephen will remain;
All he's lost he shall regain.
Sea-shore washed by the suds and the foam,
Been here so long he's got to callin' it home.

SUGAREE

Words by ROBERT HUNTER
Music by JERRY GARCIA

Sugaree - 6 - 1
PG9557

© 1971 ICE NINE PUBLISHING CO., INC.
All Rights Reserved

Verse 2:
You thought you was the cool fool,
And never could do no wrong.
You had everything sewed up tight.
How come you lay awake all night long?
(To Chorus:)

Verse 3:
Well, in spite of all you gained,
You still have to stand out in the pouring rain.
One last voice is calling you,
And I guess it's time you go.
(To Chorus:)

Verse 4:
Well, shake it up now, Sugaree,
I'll meet you at the jubilee.
And if that jubilee don't come,
Maybe I'll meet you on the run.
(To Chorus:)

TENNESSEE JED

Words by ROBERT HUNTER
Music by JERRY GARCIA

Tennessee Jed - 13 - 1
PG9557

© 1972 ICE NINE PUBLISHING CO., INC.
All Rights Reserved

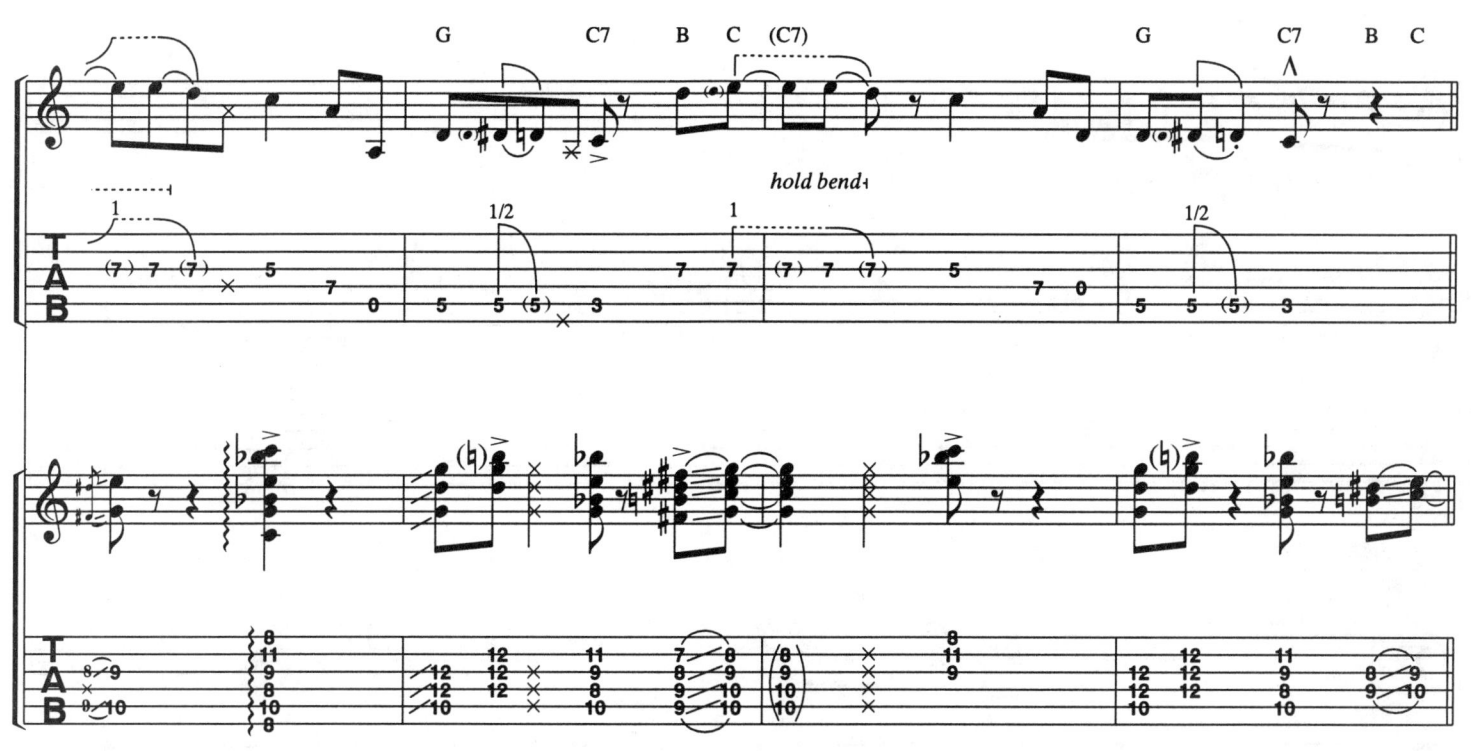

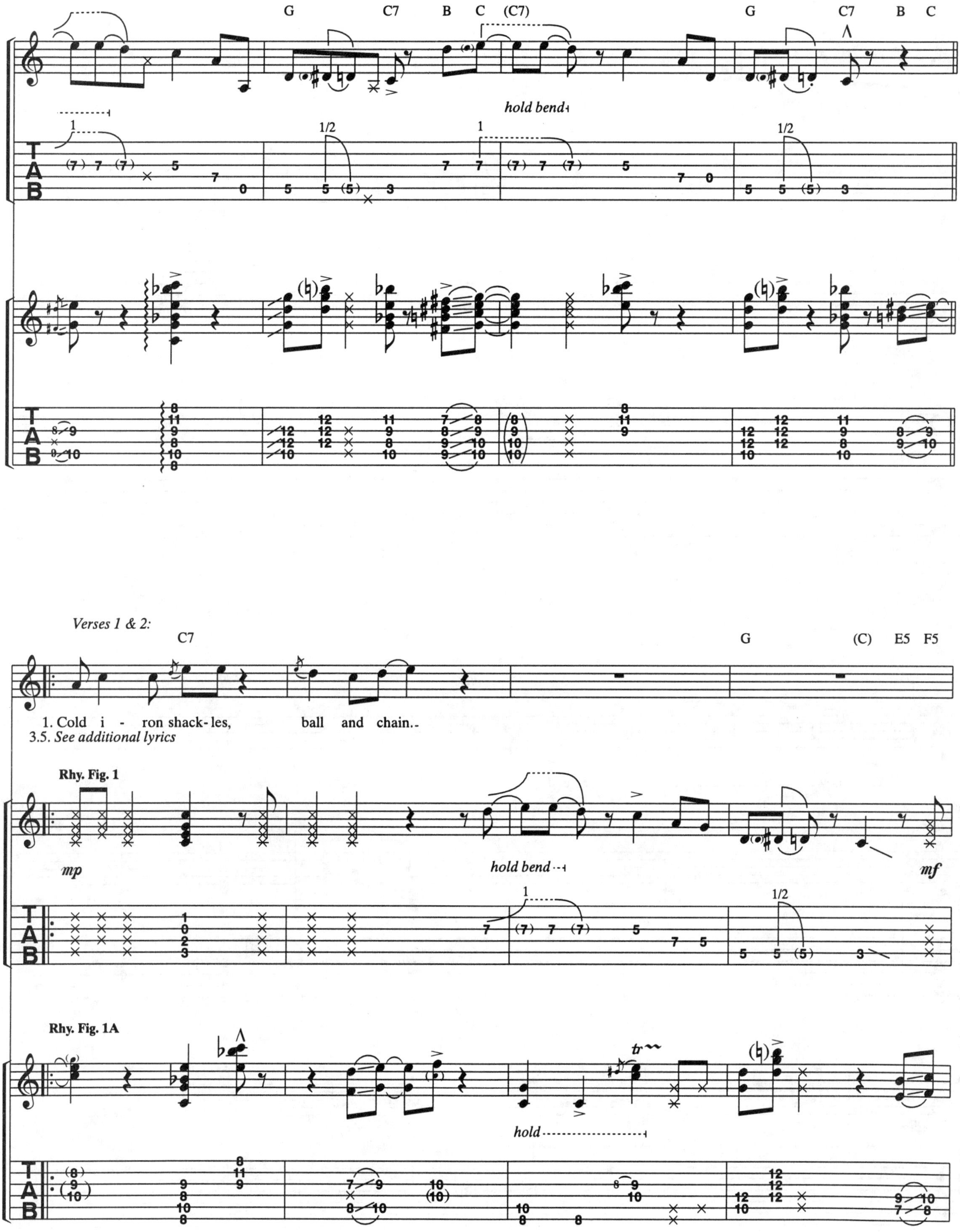
G
C7
B
C
(C7)
hold bend
Verses 1 & 2:
(C)
E5
F5
1. Cold i - ron shack- les, ball and chain.
3.5. See additional lyrics
Rhy. Fig. 1
mp
mf
Rhy. Fig. 1A
hold

G5 G6 B C G C (G)
Lis- ten to the whis- tle of the eve - nin' train.
hold bend
mf
1
1/2
hold

C Cdim7 F/A C7/G
You know you bound to wind up dead, you
hold
hold

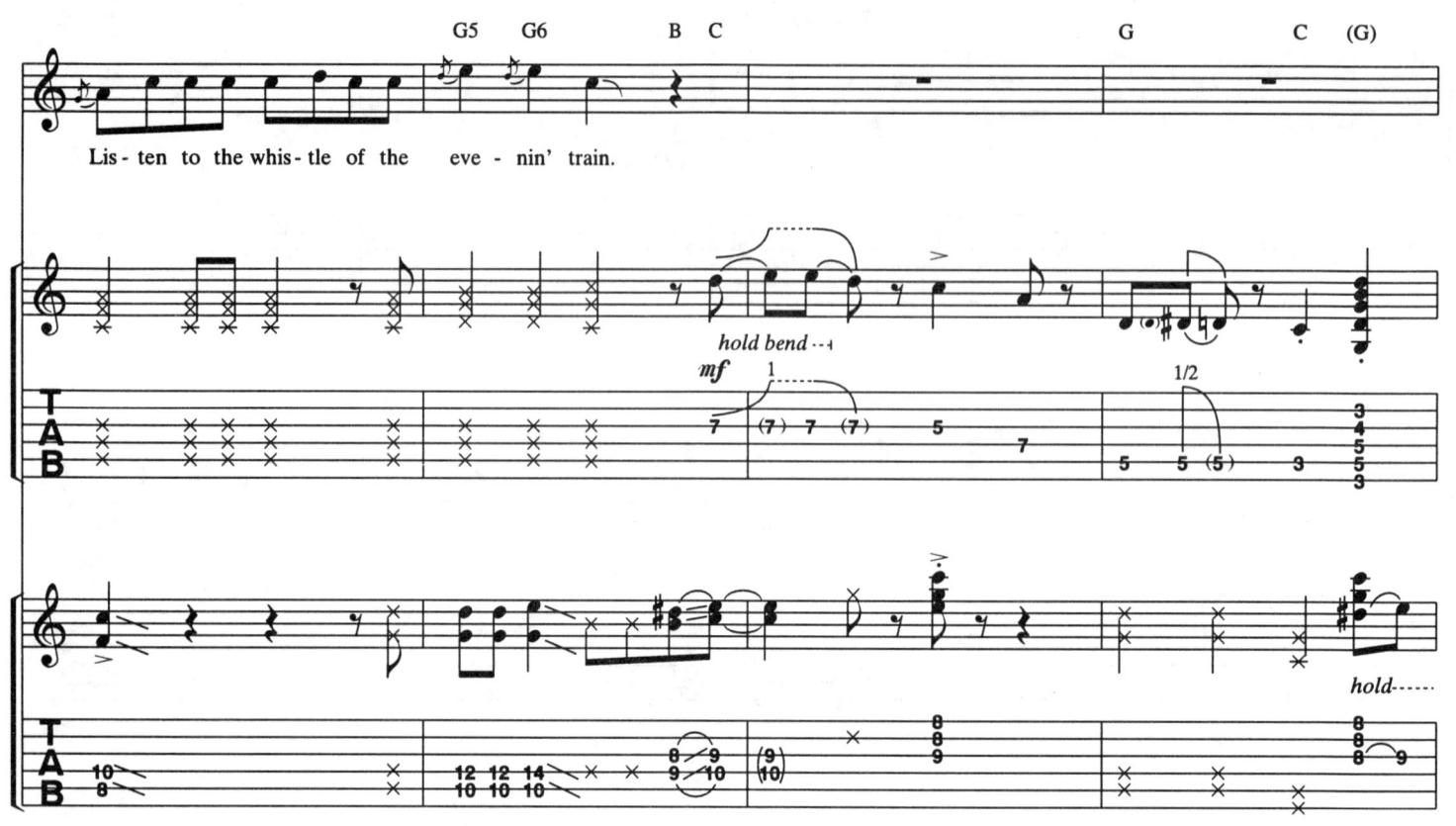

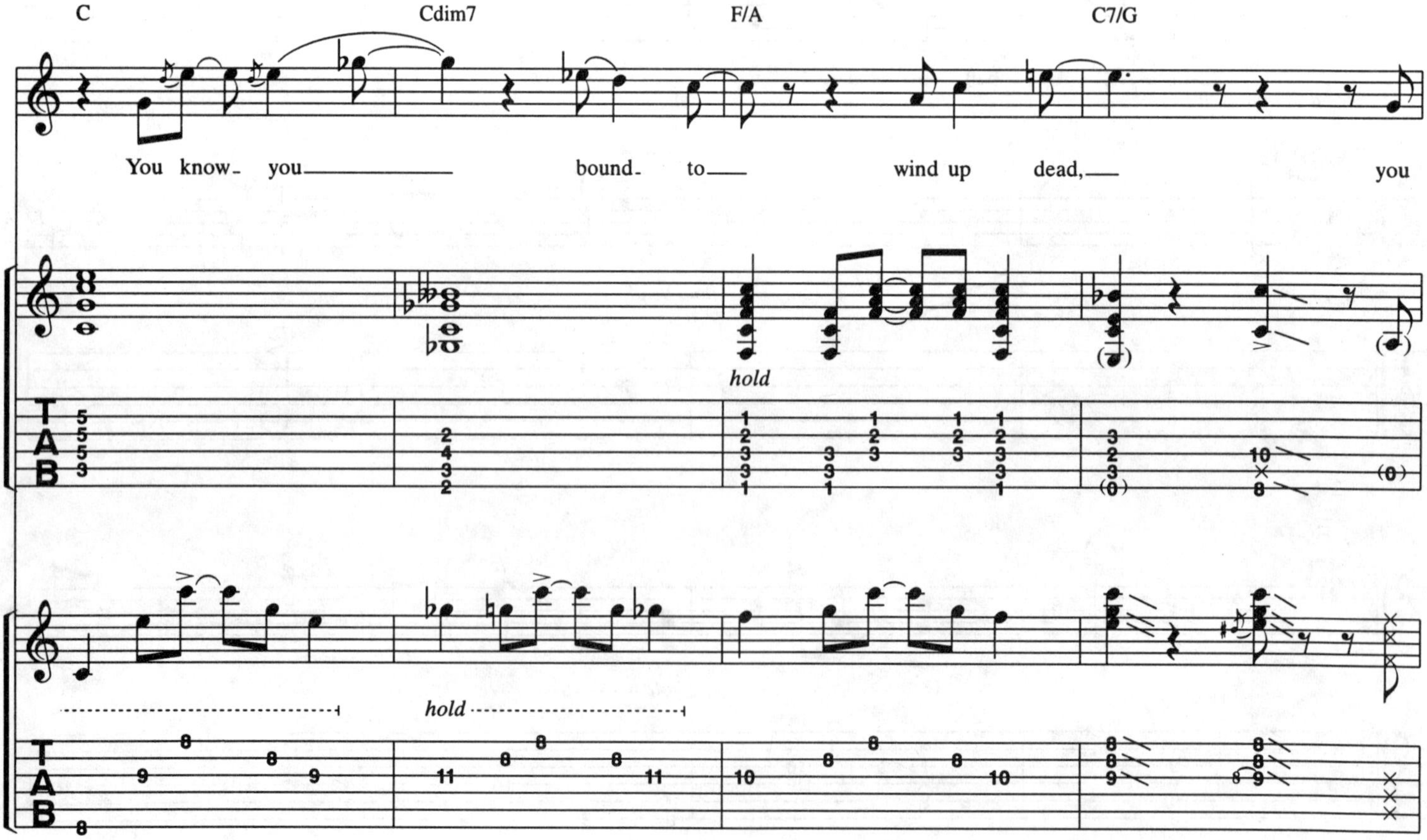

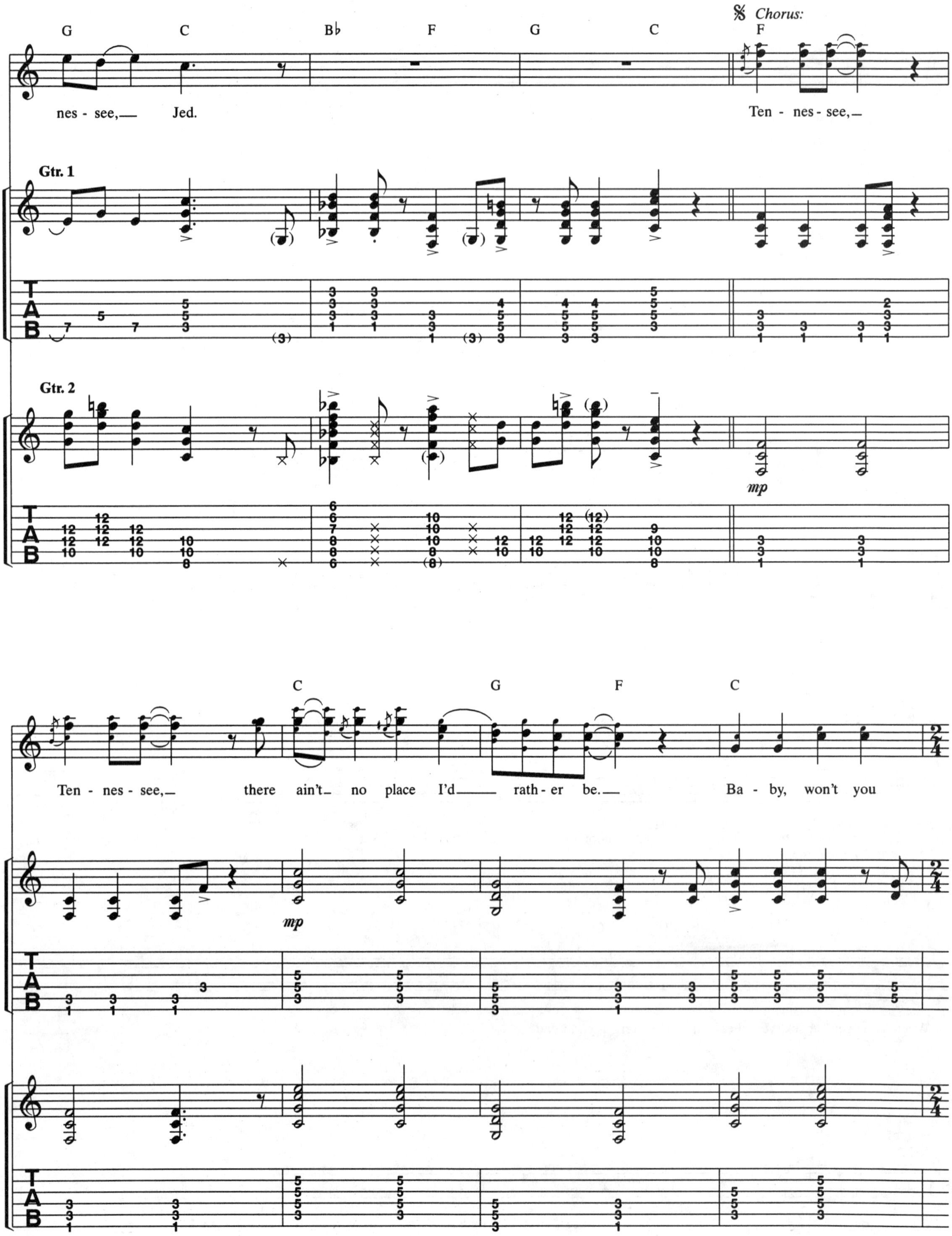

𝄋 Chorus:
G C B♭ F G C F
nes - see, Jed. Ten - nes - see,
Gtr. 1
Gtr. 2
mp
C G F C
Ten - nes - see, there ain't no place I'd rath - er be. Ba - by, won't you
mp

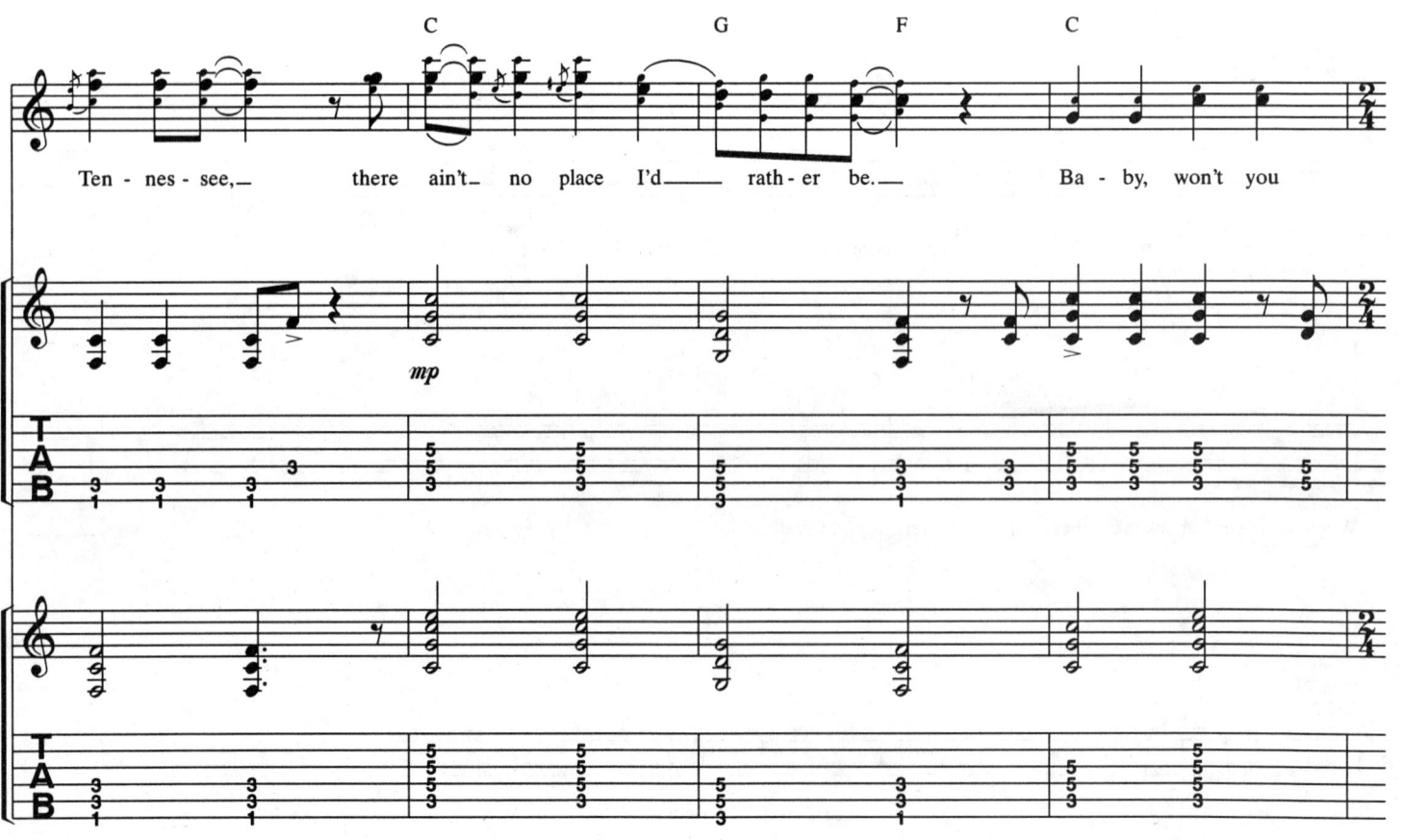

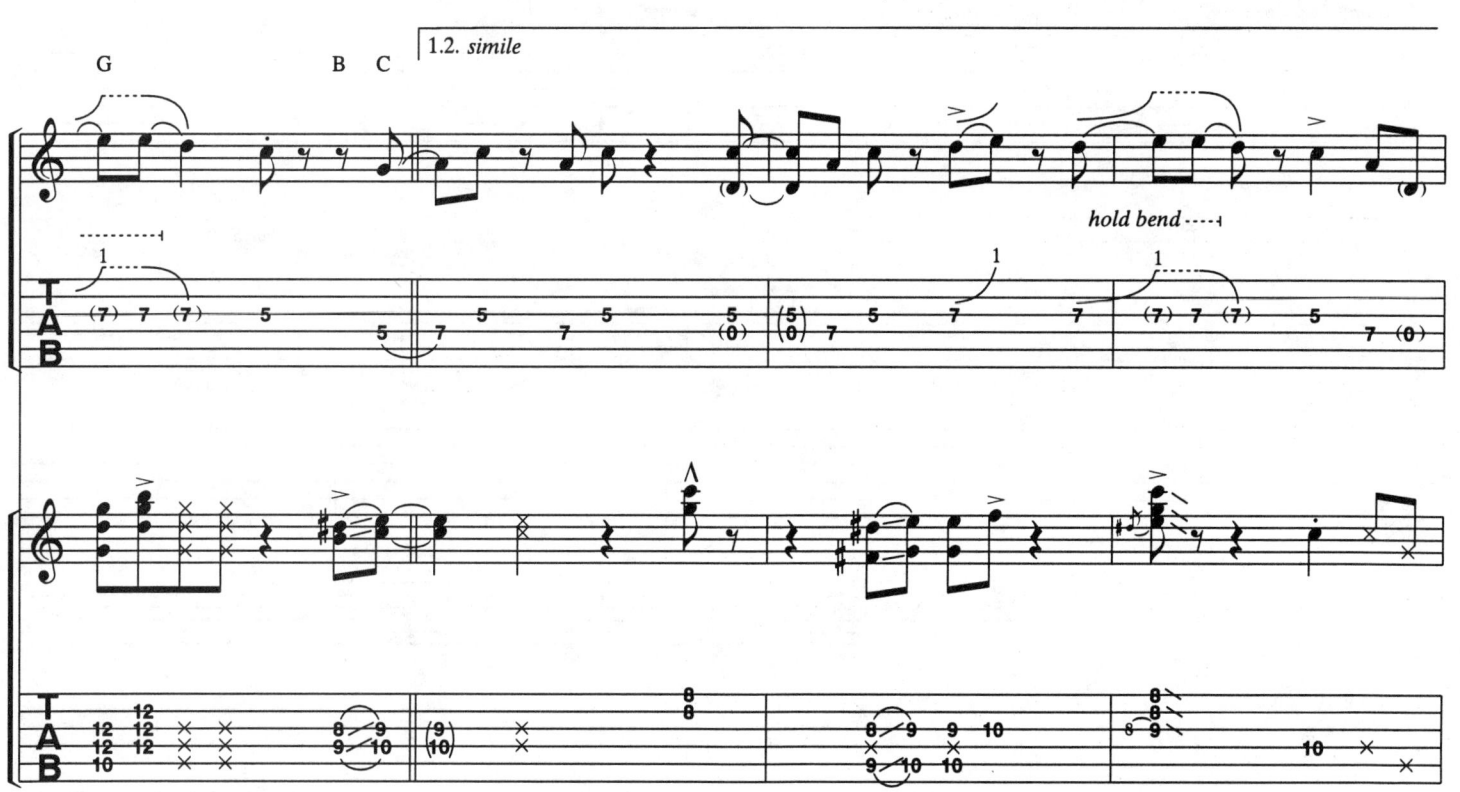

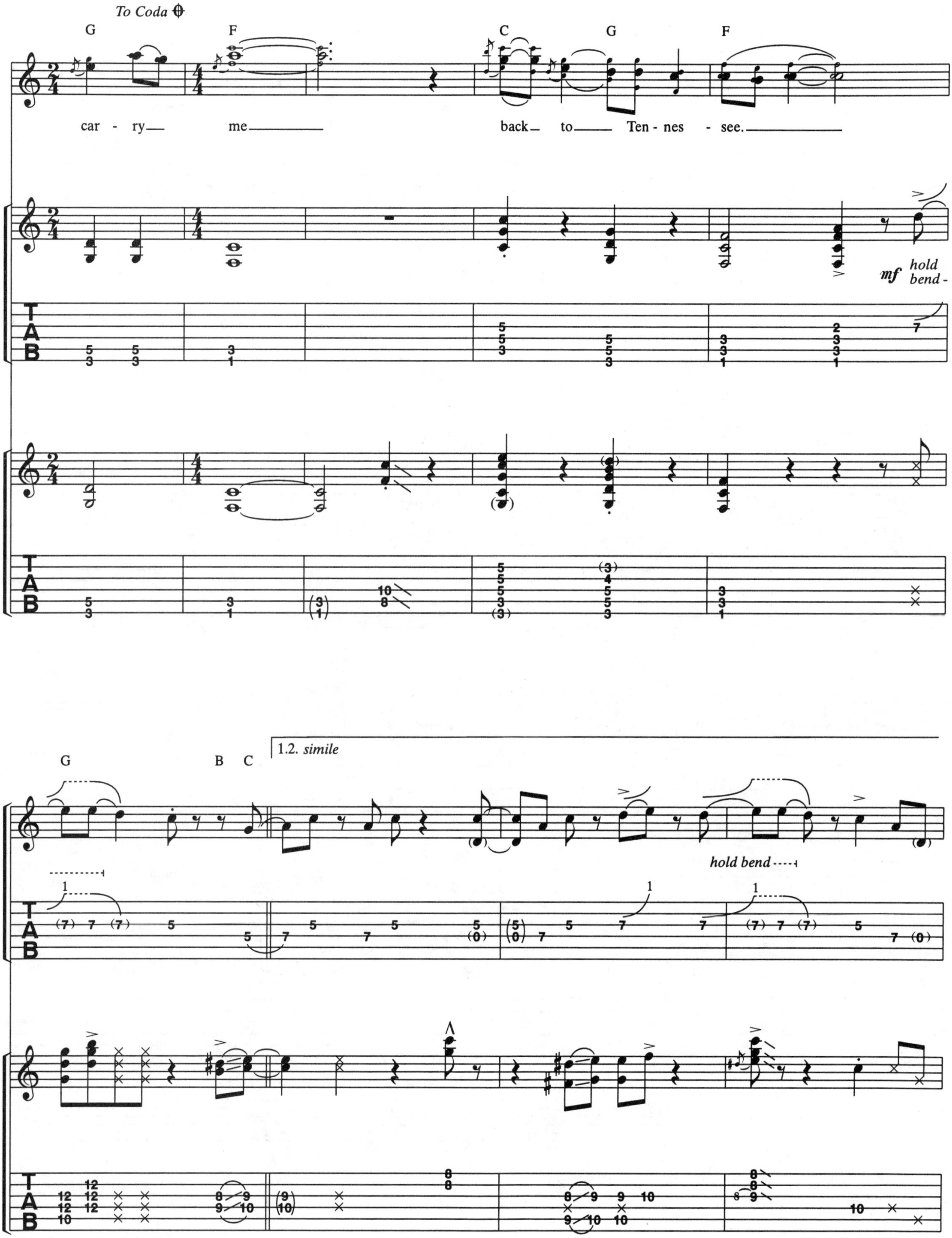
To Coda
G
F
C
G
F
car - ry me back to Ten - nes - see.
mf
hold bend -
G
B
C
1.2. simile
hold bend

118

Tennessee Jed - 13 - 7
PG9557

122

Tennessee Jed - 13 - 11
PG9557

Verse 3:
Drink all day and rock all night.
The law come to get you if you don't walk right.
Got a letter this mornin', baby.
And all it read:
"You better head back to Tennessee, Jed."

Verse 4:
I dropped four flights and cracked my spine.
Honey, come quick with the iodine.
Catch a few winks, baby, under the bed.
Then you head back to Tennessee, Jed.
(To Guitar Solo:)

Verse 5:
I run into Charlie Fog.
Blacked my eye and he kicked my dog.
My doggie turned to me and he said,
"Let's head back to Tennessee, Jed."

Verse 6:
I woke up feelin' mean.
I went down to play the slot machine.
The wheels turned around and the letters read,
"You better head back to Tennessee, Jed."
(To Coda)

TOUCH OF GREY

Words by ROBERT HUNTER
Music by JERRY GARCIA

*Bass arranged for gtr.
**Two electric gtrs. arranged for one.
***Arranged for 6 string. Sound 8va than written.

© 1984 ICE NINE PUBLISHING CO., INC.
All Rights Reserved

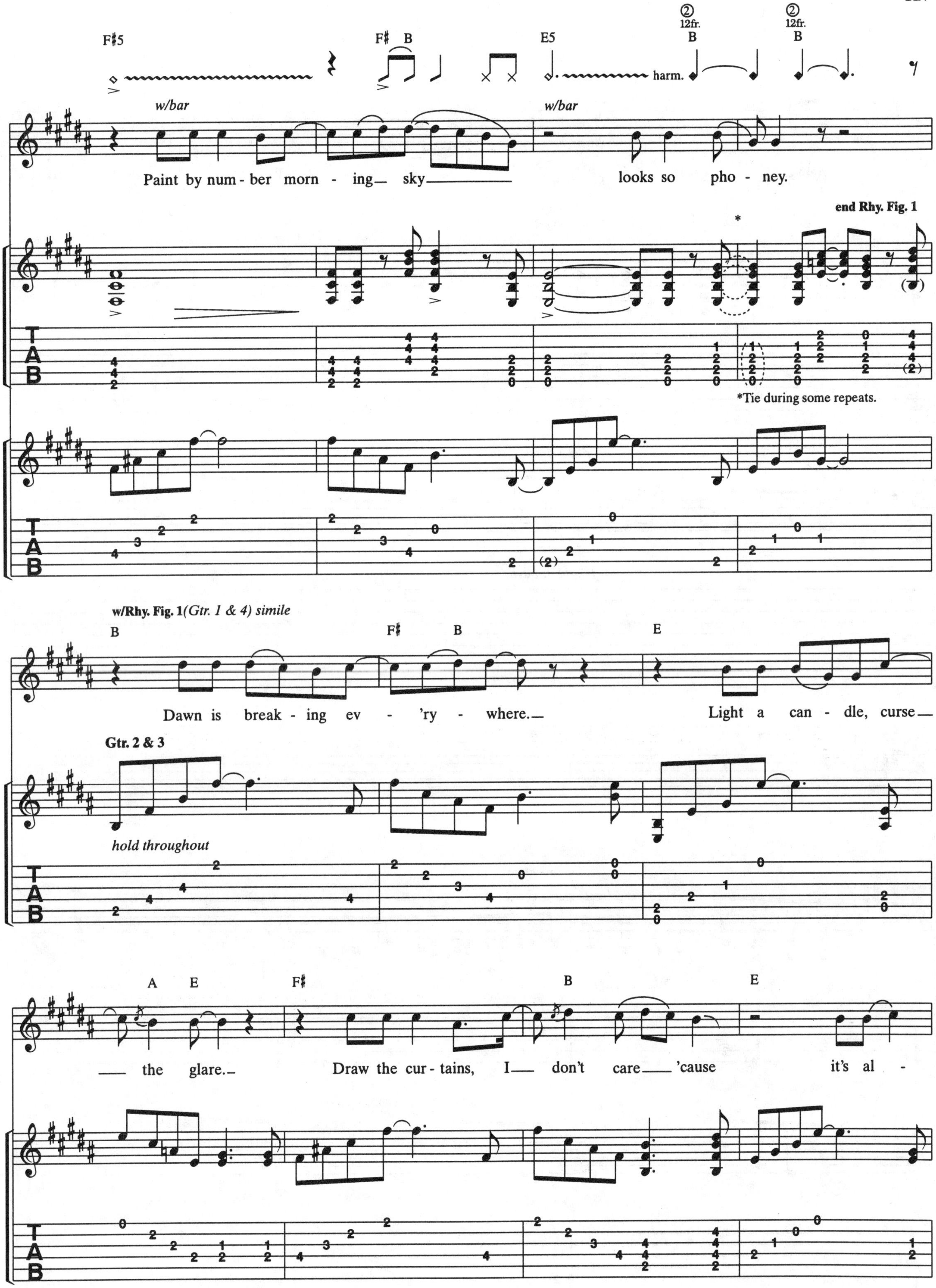
F♯5
F♯ B
E5
②
12fr.
B
harm.
w/bar
Paint by num - ber morn - ing sky
looks so pho - ney.
end Rhy. Fig. 1
*Tie during some repeats.
w/Rhy. Fig. 1 (Gtr. 1 & 4) simile
B
F♯
E
Dawn is break - ing ev - 'ry - where.
Light a can - dle, curse
Gtr. 2 & 3
hold throughout
A
the glare.
Draw the cur - tains, I don't care 'cause
it's al -

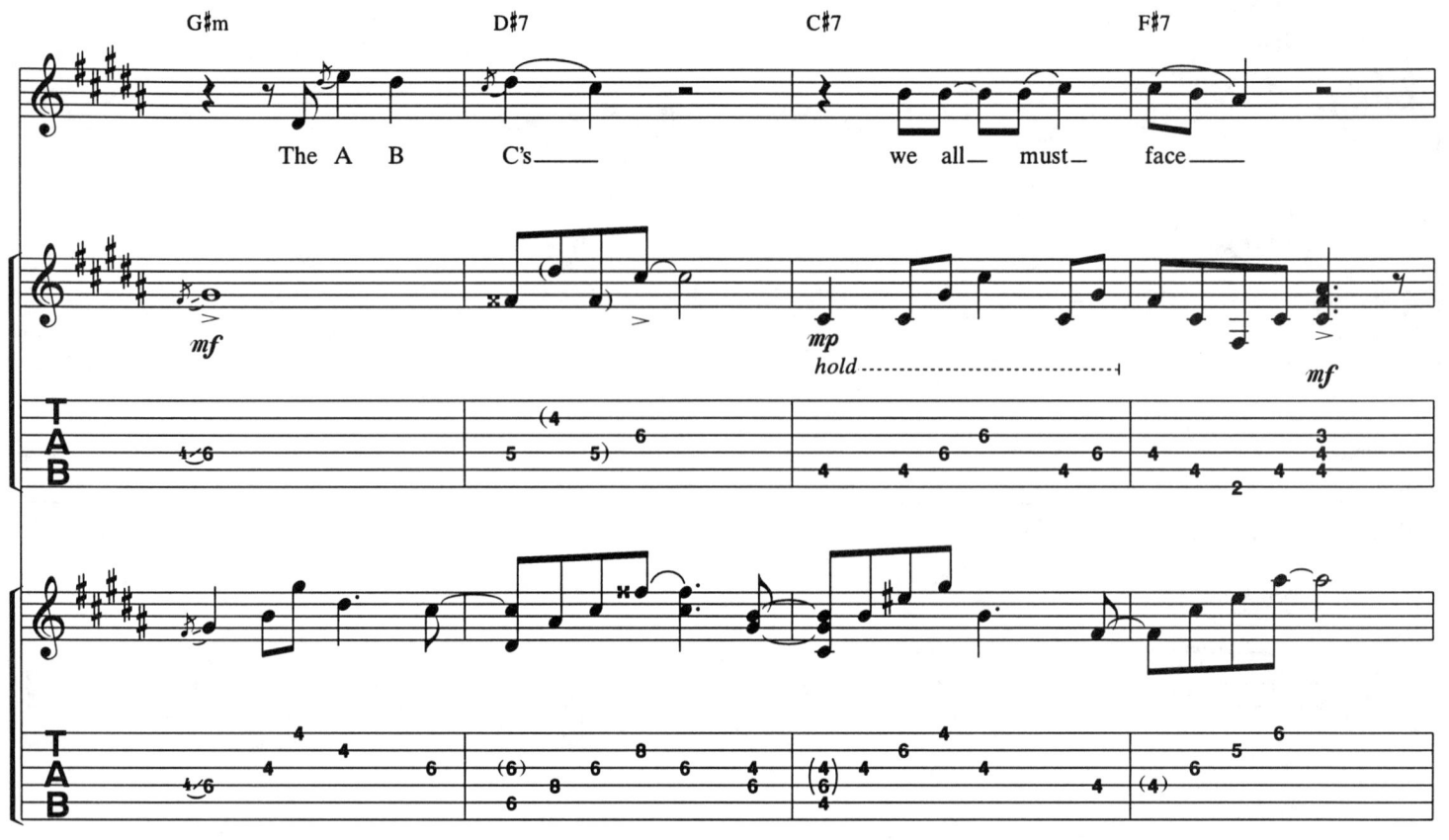

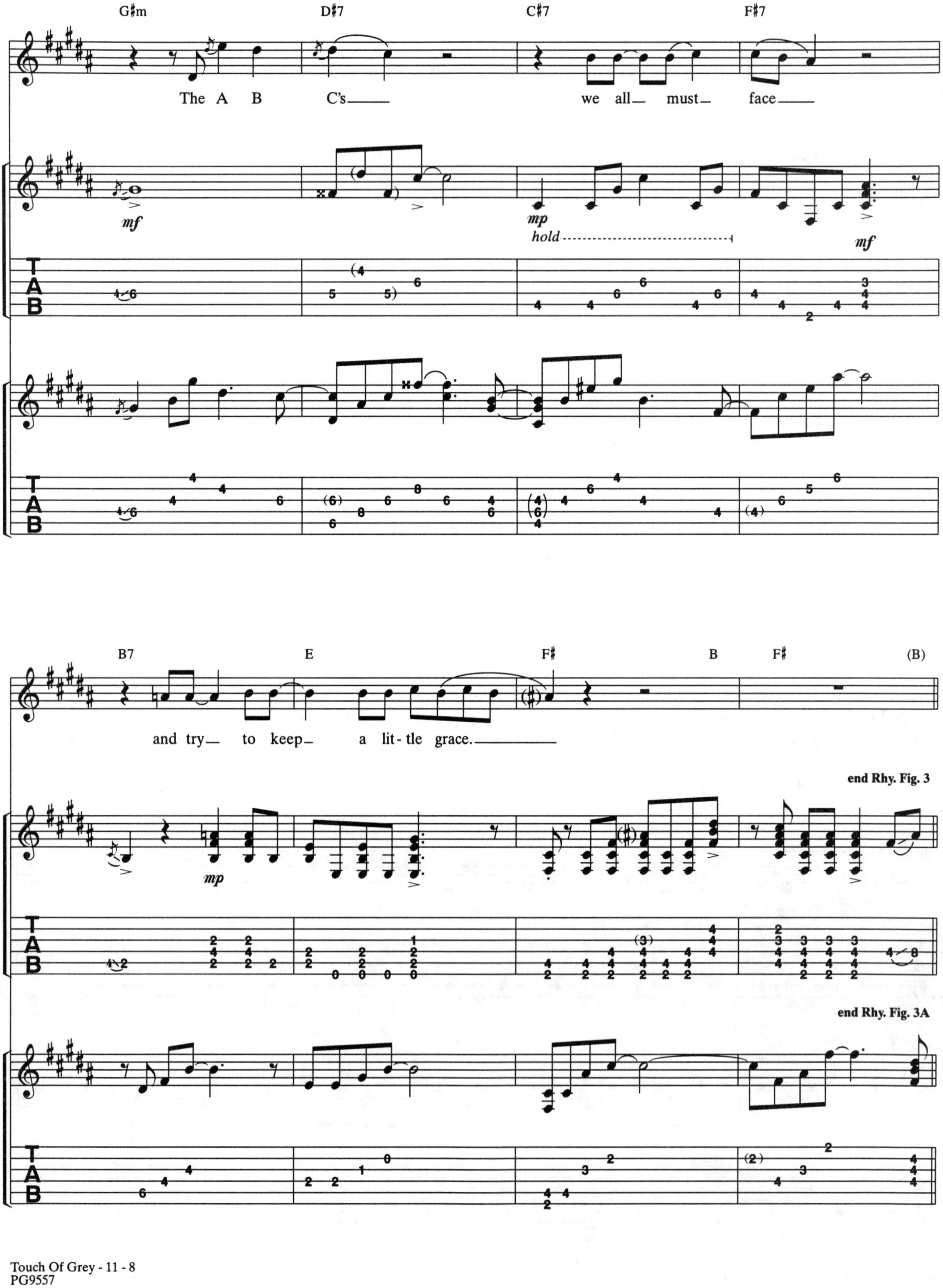
G♯m
D♯7
C♯7
F♯7
The A B C's we all must face
mf
mp
hold
mf
B7
E
F♯
B
F♯
(B)
and try to keep a lit-tle grace.
end Rhy. Fig. 3
mp
end Rhy. Fig. 3A

Verse 2:
I see you've got your list out.
Say your peace and get out.
Yes, I get the gist of it, but
It's alright.
Sorry that you feel that way.
The only thing there is to say:
Every silver lining's got a touch of grey.
(To Chorus:)

Verse 3:
I know the rent is in arrears,
The dog has not been fed in years.
It's even worse than it appears,
But it's alright.
(To Chorus:)

Verse 4:
The shoe is on the hand it fits,
There's really nothing much to it.
Whistle through your teeth and spit 'cause
It's alright.
Oh, well, a touch of grey,
Kinda suits you anyway.
That was all I had to say,
And it's alright.
(To Chorus:)

GUITAR TAB GLOSSARY **

TABLATURE EXPLANATION

READING TABLATURE: Tablature illustrates the six strings of the guitar. Notes and chords are indicated by the placement of fret numbers on a given string(s).

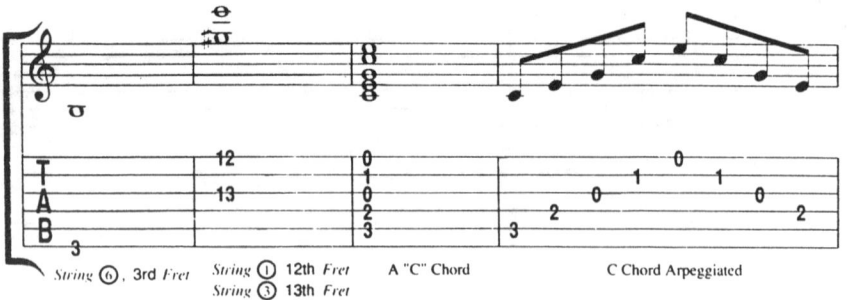

ARTICULATIONS

HAMMER ON: Play lower note, then "hammer on" to higher note with another finger. Only the first note is attacked.

PULL OFF: Play higher note, then "pull off" to lower note with another finger. Only the first note is attacked.

BENDING NOTES

HALF STEP: Play the note and bend string one half step.*

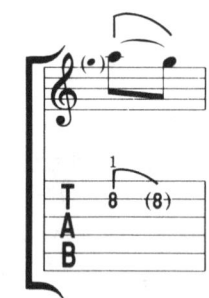

PREBEND AND RELEASE: Bend the string, play it, then release to the original note.

WHOLE STEP: Play the note and bend string one whole step.

LEGATO SLIDE: Play note and slide to the following note. (Only first note is attacked).

PALM MUTE: The note or notes are muted by the palm of the pick hand by lightly touching the string(s) near the bridge.

RHYTHM SLASHES

STRUM INDICATIONS: Strum with indicated rhythm. The chord voicings are found on the first page of the transcription underneath the song title.

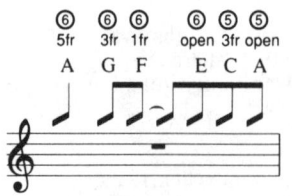

INDICATING SINGLE NOTES USING RHYTHM SLASHES: Very often single notes are incorporated into a rhythm part. The note name is indicated above the rhythm slash with a fret number and a string indication.

ACCENT: Notes or chords are to be played with added emphasis.

DOWN STROKES AND UPSTROKES: Notes or chords are to be played with either a downstroke (⊓) or upstroke (v) of the pick.

*A half step is the smallest interval in Western music; it is equal to one fret. A whole step equals two frets.

**By Kenn Chipkin and Aaron Stang

© 1990 Beam Me Up Music
c/o CPP/Belwin, Inc. Miami, Florida 33014
International Copyright Secured Made in U.S.A. All Rights Reserved